REMINISCENCES
of a
HEDGE FUND
OPERATOR

JULIAN KLYMOCHKO

Published by:

Accelerate Financial Technologies Inc.

Suite 300, 524 17 Avenue SW,

Calgary, AB T2S 0B2

1-855-892-0740

info@accelerateshares.com

Designed by Sabrina Torres
Manufactured in the United States of America and Canada

For more information, visit www.AccelerateShares.com

For enterprising investors.

Contents

1

The First Time I Lost $1 Million

The number one key to longevity in investment management is resilience to the many setbacks you'll endure.

I was 28 years old when I launched my first hedge fund in January 2012. Prior to that, I had co-managed a systematic market neutral hedge fund for a few years. A number of wealthy investors decided to back my new fund to the tune of $5 million to run a risk arbitrage strategy, which bets on mergers, acquisitions, takeovers, liquidations, bankruptcies, and other event-driven trades.

As a young hedge fund manager eager to prove my skills, I did everything I could to make the fund a success. I set my daily alarm to 4:00 am and was in the office every day by 5:00 am. Evening, weekend, and holiday work was a must. I was even at my Bloomberg terminal every Sunday evening, preparing for Monday's trading session.

For the first four months, I woke up sick to my stomach every morning. The pressure was intense. Nonetheless, I worked through it, focused on my goal of becoming a successful hedge fund manager.

Off To A Good Start

The first year went about as good as one could hope for. The fund finished its inaugural year up 11.4%, net of its 2% management fee and 20% performance fee. It attained this return with only three down months, the worst of which was

-1.1%. The fund achieved this return with an annualized standard deviation of only 4.1%. Its Sharpe ratio, a measure of reward per unit of risk, was near 3.

Things continued to go well for the fund. After 32 months, we were compounding at nearly 10% annualized (net of fees) with a standard deviation of less than 4%. We were showing investors steady gains with low volatility with our risk arbitrage investment strategy. Money came flowing in from new investors and the fund grew sixfold. Our strategy was working. Everything was going right.

It's All Over

In September 2014, the honeymoon ended. We had a merger arbitrage trade on to profit from Auxilium Pharmaceuticals' friendly acquisition of QLT Inc. Back in June 2014, Auxilium struck a friendly deal to acquire QLT in an all-share deal at a 25% premium. An arbitrageur could profit from the deal by buying QLT stock and shorting Auxilium stock to earn the arbitrage spread that existed between the two securities. We held a large position in the merger arbitrage trade for the fund, consisting of a long position in QLT and a short position in Auxilium.

3

The worst thing that could ever happen to a merger arbitrageur is when an interloper submits an unsolicited offer for the acquiror (i.e., the stock you are short) in a merger arbitrage trade. Not only would you lose money on your short position, which would rally against you, but you'd also lose money on your long target position, which would plummet as the deal broke.

Merger arbitrage requires stringent risk management. You're always thinking about what could go wrong. I played out all the potential scenarios in which the QLT / Auxilium deal could break. Could Auxilium itself attract takeover interest? Not with its current product suite (don't research Auxilium's product, and if you do, definitely don't Google it). I thought Auxilium was fundamentally not an attractive acquisition candidate.

However, I had an inkling in the back of my mind that there was a tiny risk that an interloper could make a hostile play for Auxilium. A merger mania was taking place in the pharmaceuticals sector in 2014. Industry giant, Valeant Pharmaceuticals, run by CEO Mike Pearson, was seemingly buying every company in sight. Endo International, another deal-hungry pharmaceutical company run by Mike Pearson-protégé Rajiv De Silva, was also pursuing an aggressive acquisition strategy.

I couldn't shake the feeling that one of these deal junkies could potentially make a play for Auxilium, despite what I viewed as poor fundamentals that would make it an unattractive acquisition candidate. We began buying call options on Auxilium to protect the fund in the scenario in which Auxilium caught a hostile bid.

After the market close on September 16, 2014, disaster struck. Endo announced an unsolicited proposal to acquire for Auxilium at a 30.6% premium. This was the worst possible scenario for the fund. On Endo's conference call to discuss the deal, CEO De Silva indicated that the offer was contingent on Auxilium dropping its acquisition of QLT. It was clear that Endo's offer killed the QLT / Auxilium deal in which we had a sizeable position.

Getting My Face Ripped Off

The market reaction was swift. The next day, our long position, QLT, tanked -13.1%. Making matters much, much worse, we had our face ripped off with our Auxilium short position, which skyrocketed nearly 45%. We simply didn't buy enough of the call options to protect ourselves under this scenario. Ouch!

This was the worst day of my career, by far. I ran the numbers – I had lost my investors $1 million that day. Ironically, the term Auxilium is Latin for "help", and I sure needed it.

The fund finished September down -3%. This was nearly triple the fund's previous worst monthly performance of -1.1%. While stock market investors wouldn't sweat a -3% drawdown, our investors were conditioned for steady gains.

When our investors received their monthly statements, they were angry. We hosted a conference call to talk with investors through what happened. Investors were livid and yelled at me. I felt like an idiot! My jerk of a brain told me, "Well you had a good run, kid. You're done!"

I wasn't done. The fund scratched and clawed its way back to finish the year up 4.2%. We followed that mediocre performance with a 10.9% annual gain in 2015 along with an award from BarclayHedge for a top event-driven fund for 2015.

Mistakes Were Made

What happened to Endo, the company that almost put an early end to my career?

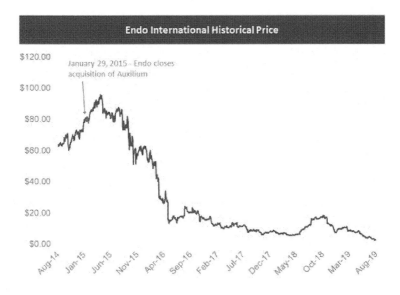

Source: Accelerate, Bloomberg

In the five years since Endo announced the acquisition of Auxilium, Endo has had over $3 billion in goodwill impairment charges (write-downs of its acquisitions). Its stock is down -97%, representing a loss of $12 billion in market value. Endo's $2.6 billion acquisition of Auxilium closed in January 2015 and by November 2015, it wrote off

7

$531 million of Auxilium's value[1]. It's fair to say Endo's consolidation strategy did not work out and its acquisition of Auxilium was ill-advised. The deal shouldn't have happened, but it did, and I learned a painful lesson.

Auxilium Taught Me

If you're an investor, you will face setbacks. It is inevitable. You have to roll with the punches. The number one key to longevity in investment management is resilience to the many setbacks you'll endure. Over time, a hedge fund manager accumulates battle scars – some memorable, and some forgotten. The first time I lost $1 million will always stick with me.

---

[1]Sec. *"Frequently Asked Questions & Answers,"* Bloomberg LP, 2018, https://www.sec.gov/Archives/edgar/data/1593034/00011931251537100 5/d81465dex992.htm

2

Embracing the Suck

This is the cost of building long-term wealth.

"Embracing the suck" refers to consciously accepting or appreciating a future event that is extremely unpleasant and uncomfortable but ultimately unavoidable. The phrase is often used in the military to encourage troops to have a positive attitude and manage expectations regarding the inevitable stress-causing events one comes across in military life. Athletes use it as well to endure and work through the intense physical and mental stress it takes to build one's body into peak physical shape.

No Pain, No Gain

Markets can be volatile - sometimes, gut-wrenchingly so. As of this writing, the S&P 500 is down over -16% since its recent peak. Nearly half of global stock markets are in bear market territory (down -20% or more).

Regular stock market corrections, the occasional bear market, and the rare market crash are all par for the course when investing. Sure, these things suck, but must be embraced if one is to enjoy the fruits of long-term compounding of wealth in the stock market.

> "Sell Everything and Run for Your Lives"
> - Société Générale strategist, October 2014

No matter what, there will always be a market prognosticator who will tell you how bad of an idea it is to hold stocks, how the market is going to crash, and to sell everything now (they're known as "perma-bears"). They'll have impressive credentials, substantial market experience, and they'll come across as extremely intelligent. Occasionally they'll be right (as a broken clock sometimes is), but they will be wrong the vast majority of the time.

The thing is, no one in the history of markets has correctly timed selling every market top and buying every market bottom. While those who sold in summer 2008 looked like geniuses a year later, they likely didn't buy back in at the bottom in 2009 (or ever), and the constant buying and selling since at the hint of any trouble has only reduced their long-term returns.

Let's not kid ourselves, it's unpleasant to see your portfolio and net worth decline markedly. You work hard for your money, and you want to see your savings go up over time. Watching your portfolio get pummeled seems like a setback - all that hard work undone.

The only way to get around these downdrafts in your portfolio is to stick with short-term government debt securities, which typically yield around 1%-2%. While everyone is different, for most investors this 1%-2% per year return is insufficient to meet their long-term financial goals.

To enjoy the stock market's long-term average 7% return (and potentially higher for hedge funds and private equity), one must embrace and accept the fact that there will be some bumps along the way.

You Gotta Be In It To Win It

I had the pleasure of holding a portfolio of stocks during the great financial crisis of 2008; even watching my entire portfolio drop by double digits some days. It was distressing to go through, especially for a young person with modest savings and only a couple years into my career. But those with the intestinal fortitude to buy stocks when the market was crashing were rewarded handsomely, with many stocks going up 5x-10x (or more) in the ensuing rebound.

Ever wish you bought Amazon stock in its IPO and held to this today? Sure, you'd likely be a multimillionaire. But you would have had to suffer through jarring volatility that would test even the most determined of investors. In addition to a number of more than -50% declines, Amazon's stock dropped a stunning -95% after the tech bubble burst. Most investors do not have the fortitude to handle this sort of decline and that's why Jeff Bezos is the world's richest man. Japan's richest, Masayoshi Son, watched his net worth decline -99% in the early 2000's. Good thing he has the resilience to follow a 300-year plan [2].

Over the long run, the stock market can make investors rich. But if it were easy, everyone would do it. Sustaining large drawdowns in net worth and having the intestinal fortitude to not panic sell at the bottom is the price of admission in getting rich.

> *"...you can argue that if you're not willing to react with equanimity to a market price decline of 50% two or three times a century you're not fit to be a common shareholder, and you deserve the mediocre result you're going to get compared to the people who do have the temperament, who can be more philosophical about these market fluctuations."*
> - Berkshire Hathaway Vice Chairman Charlie Munger

---

[2] Barr, Alistair & Newcomer, Eric. *"SoftBank CEO Adds Driverless Tech to 300-Year Plan with GM Deal,"* Bloomberg LP, 2018, https://www.bloomberg.com/news/articles/2018-05-31/gm-driverless-car-deal-adds-to-softbank-chief-s-300-year-plan

Embracing the suck can be a badge of honour and a testament to the dedication of those who adopt it. You're far better off just embracing the suck in the markets and holding long term, recognizing that the market on average tends to drop -10% every year, -20% every handful of years and over -50% at least a couple times in your investing lifetime. This is the cost of building long-term wealth.

3
Risk Management, Before it's Too Late

A long-term, pre-planned asset allocation framework can help manage risks before adverse volatility hits.

Risk management is an important aspect of investment portfolio construction. However, this much-needed protection against adversity is rarely implemented before it's too late.

Unfortunately, instead of a well-thought-out and implemented risk management plan, many investors are stuck panicking after a large market drawdown and some even end up capitulating and selling their investments at the lows, realizing significant losses and interrupting their long-term investment goals. These spooked investors remain out of the market, unable to capitalize on the bounce back in asset values.

Instead of worrying about risk management when it's too late, the best approach is to plan ahead. And the best way to manage risk before the turbulence hits is through diversification.

Diversification is a risk management technique that combines a wide variety of investments within a portfolio. The purpose of true diversification is to hold a myriad of asset classes that don't move in the same direction as each other (i.e., being uncorrelated).

This pre-planned diversification has another term: *Asset allocation*.

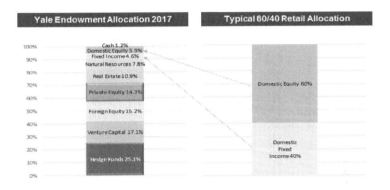

Source: Accelerate, Yale Endowment

How do the top institutional investors in the world approach asset allocation? Let's take a look at the Yale University endowment [3] for guidance:

As you can see, Yale's asset allocation (i.e., diversified portfolio) varies dramatically from the standard 60% / 40% mix of stocks and bonds typically recommended to average investors.

---

[3] "The Yale Endowment 2017," 2017,
https://static1.squarespace.com/static/55db7b87e4b0dca22fba2438/t/5a
c5890e758d4611a98edd15/1522895146491/Yale_Endowment_17.pdf

In fact, instead of a 60% allocation to domestic stocks, Yale only has a 3.9% allocation. Instead of a 40% allocation to domestic bonds, Yale only has a 4.6% allocation.

What's Going On Here?

Yale is viewed as the "gold standard" in asset allocation and is led by legendary investor David Swensen. It has achieved remarkable, long-term success in investing. In his own words:

> "During the decade ending June 30, 2017, Yale's investment program added $5.3 billion of value relative to the results of the mean endowment. The University's 20-year market-leading return of 12.1 percent per annum produced $24.3 billion in relative value. Over the past 30 years, Yale's investments have returned an unparalleled 12.5 percent per annum, adding $28.0 billion in value relative to the Cambridge mean. Sensible long-term investment policies, grounded by a commitment to equities and a belief in diversification, underpin the University's investment success."

The more diversified asset allocation of Yale's endowment, with healthy allocations to alternative strategies, helped produce market-beating long-term returns.

Yale currently has a significant portion of its assets invested in alternative strategies; 25% allocated to hedge funds (also known as Absolute Return strategies) and 14% allocated to private equity.

When seeking to further diversify your portfolio and manage risk before it's too late, look to the "gold standard" of asset allocators. Consider going beyond just stocks and bonds and investigate whether alternatives, such as hedge funds and private equity strategies, are right for your portfolio.

A long-term, pre-planned asset allocation framework can help manage risks before adverse volatility hits.

4

Sentiment is Path-Dependent

The recency bias has a tremendous effect on investors' sentiment, which in turn has a substantial effect on investment decisions.

There was a popular, speculative asset that was down - 74.3% in 2018 and the *schadenfreude* was off the charts.

Over any reasonable time frame to judge the merits of an investment (>5 years), this asset has provided investors with exceptional returns. In fact, it is certainly one of the best-performing assets in the world over the past seven years. If this asset were bought at the end of 2011, it would have realized nearly a 1,000x return and a $10,000 investment would have turned into almost $9 million. A 162.5% compound annual growth rate (CAGR) over seven years is an extremely rare and exceptional investment.

Returns to December 31, 2018				
Start Date	Years	CAGR	Total Return	Growth of $10,000
19-Jul-10	8.5	255.8%	4,592,625.0%	$459,272,500
30-Dec-11	7.0	162.5%	86,351.3%	$8,645,129
31-Dec-13	5.0	37.5%	391.9%	$49,193
31-Dec-14	4.0	84.4%	1,057.7%	$115,773
31-Dec-15	3.0	104.0%	750.3%	$85,029
30-Dec-16	2.0	96.3%	285.9%	$38,594
29-Dec-17	1.0	-74.1%	-74.3%	$2,567

Source: Bloomberg

This asset was down big over the past year and the market is swift with its pronouncements - any asset that has suffered poor performance over the recent near term gets criticized as a scam at worst or overvalued at best, irrespective of long-term price performance or underlying intrinsic value.

Cognitive BIAS

This is irrational behaviour is driven by a cognitive bias called the recency effect. A cognitive bias refers to an error in thinking that humans make when processing information. *Recency BIAS* The recency bias dictates that people give greater importance to recent information than to data from further in the past.

Nobel Prize winning psychologist Daniel Kahneman wrote a best-selling book titled, *Thinking Fast and Slow*, in which he details two ways the human brain forms thoughts:

1. System 1 - Fast, emotional and intuitive decision making that tends to be completed often without much thought, such as calculating 2 x 2 in your head.
2. System 2 - Slow, effortful, calculating and rational decision making that is rare and requires concentration, such as calculating 13 x 23 in your head.

Kahneman's main point is that the human brain can be lazy and commit certain cognitive biases when it utilizes system 1 (fast thinking) instead of system 2 (slow thinking).

Let's take a look at the price action of the reference asset:

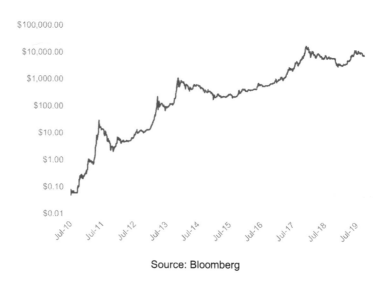

Source: Bloomberg

Since this asset was down -74.3% over the past year, a soul-crushing drawdown by any measure, the market is extremely pessimistic on its prospects. But this pessimism is driven entirely by the recent price action.

But say the recent price action was only slightly different - say the asset *only* increased by +100% in 2017 (instead of rocketing up +285.9%), and ended up at the same place on December 31, 2018. This asset would have recorded a +93% return for 2018 and sentiment would have been off-the-charts positive. The only difference is we ignored the asset's increase in value for the second half of 2017.

So, we have two scenarios with the same asset at the same ending price but both likely having dramatically different sentiment. The current path providing extremely bearish sentiment, while the path-tweaked asset likely enjoying tremendously bullish sentiment.

The recency bias has a tremendous effect on investors' sentiment, which in turn has a substantial effect on investment decisions.

It is important to be aware of these inherent cognitive biases that the vast majority of investors suffer.

Combat the recency bias by putting additional weight to other factors such as valuation and long-term asset performance, instead of making a fast, system 1 decision based on recent price action.

Think slow.

5

The Danger of Return Targeting

Blindly following a return target, while it becomes increasingly difficult to reach, is perhaps irresponsible when you have no choice but to increase allocations to one of the riskiest asset classes.

Pension funds are some of the most sophisticated investors in the market. These funds represent enormous pools of capital, some larger than $100 billion, so their resources are near limitless and they are typically run by the best and brightest.

Pension funds function by taking in contributions from workers, investing this capital on behalf of these pension plan participants, and earning an adequate return on these investments to be able to pay these workers the promised amount, known as pension obligations, once they retire.

Major pension plans have historically made some pretty sweet promises to their workers with respect to their defined retirement benefits, and therefore need to earn a certain targeted investment return in order to meet these lofty expectations and significant pension obligations.

One of the largest pension funds out there, the $356 billion California Public Employees' Retirement System (Calpers), has a 7% return target [4].

These targeted returns, a necessary yardstick that pension funds need to meet the promised obligations to current and

---

[4] "A Solid Foundation for the Future," CalPERS, 2019, https://www.calpers.ca.gov/page/about/organization/facts-at-a-glance/solid-foundation-for-the-future

future pensioners, were initially set decades ago as a relatively modest target to achieve.

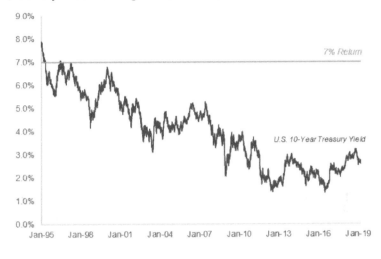

Source: Bloomberg

Over the last few decades, investors needing a certain target return have had an increasingly difficult time reaching those targets. This is due to the steady decline in long-term bond yields over the years. A generation ago, these target returns could be attained through a simple allocation to 10-year U.S. Treasury bonds. Long-term pension spending obligations were set when high returns were readily attainable with much lower risk.

For example, in 1995, a 7.5% return target could be attained through a portfolio of 100% bonds. This all-bond portfolio was relatively low risk, with a standard deviation of 6%.

Bonds are typically the safest portion of an investment portfolio.

With the precipitous decline of long-term bond yields over the past four decades, by 2015, an investor needed a much more aggressive portfolio to attain those same 7.5% returns. By 2015, the 7.5% return target portfolio had a bond allocation of only 12%. In its place, a mix of higher-risk stocks, real estate, and private equity. This higher-risk portfolio has a standard deviation, commonly viewed as risk, of 17.2%, nearly triple the amount of volatility as the all-bond portfolio from 1995 that accomplished equivalent returns.

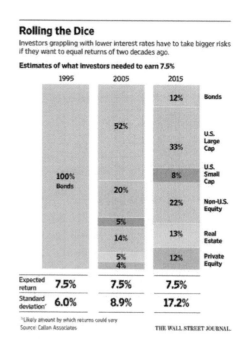

Rolling the Dice

Investors grappling with lower interest rates have to take bigger risks if they want to equal returns of two decades ago.

Estimates of what investors needed to earn 7.5%

	1995	2005	2015	
			12%	Bonds
		52%		
			33%	U.S. Large Cap
	100% Bonds		8%	U.S. Small Cap
		20%		
			22%	Non-U.S. Equity
		5%		
		14%	13%	Real Estate
		5%	12%	Private Equity
		4%		
Expected return	7.5%	7.5%	7.5%	
Standard deviation*	6.0%	8.9%	17.2%	

*Likely amount by which returns could vary
Source: Callan Associates   THE WALL STREET JOURNAL.

As you could probably guess, tripling the risk level of a portfolio is a dangerous proposition.

The Calpers transcript from its February 2019 investment committee meeting is a worthwhile read. In the meeting, Calpers Chief Investment Officer Ben Meng reveals an alarming thought (emphasis mine):

> "*So, if I could give you a one line exact summary of this entire presentation would be **we need private equity, we need more of it, and we need it now**. So, let's talk about the first question, why do we need private equity? And the answer is very simple, **to increase our chance of achieving the seven percent rate of return**.*"
>
> -Calpers Chief Investment Officer Ben Meng, Calpers Investment Committee Open Session [5]

Private equity is one of the riskiest asset classes. For example, the Yale endowment [6] estimates private equity's standard deviation at 23.6%. Its estimated risk level for

---

[5] Peters, James. "Public Employees' Retirement System Board of Administration Investment Committee Open Session," CalPERS, 2019, https://www.calpers.ca.gov/docs/board-agendas/201902/invest/transcript-ic_a.pdf

[6] "The Yale Endowment 2017," 2017, https://static1.squarespace.com/static/55db7b87e4b0dca22fba2438/t/5ac5890e758d4611a98edd15/1522895146491/Yale_Endowment_17.pdf

private equity is over 30% higher than that of domestic equities at 18% and nearly triple the risk level of hedge funds at 8.6%.

No wonder private equity is expected to have higher returns. It is a highly risky investment strategy - significantly riskier than being long the S&P 500. Private equity is no panacea. Empirical evidence shows [7] that private equity return profiles are equivalent to that of a portfolio of small-cap, low EBITDA-multiple stocks with leverage.

Given this notion, it is frightening to see a pension fund needing to ramp up its risk appetite in order to meet increasingly lofty return ambitions, with little to no concern for risk. The thing about leverage, private equity's "secret sauce", is that it cuts both ways. It amplifies positive returns to the upside and it also magnifies investment losses to the downside.

Private equity is illiquid and typically "marked to model". It does not have to stand up to the daily judgement of an unforgiving stock market. Because it doesn't get marked-to-market on a daily basis, doesn't mean an investor can be

---

[7] Stafford, Erik. "Replicating Private Equity with Value Investing, Homemade Leverage, and Hold-to-Maturity Accounting," Harvard Business School, 2015, https://www.hbs.edu/faculty/Publication%20Files/ReplicatingPE_201512_3859877f-bd53-4d3e-99aa-6daec2a3a2d3.pdf

oblivious to its volatility. The fact is that private equity is over 30% more volatile than U.S. stocks, given private equity's propensity for leveraged equities. When the stock market is down -20%, you can expect a private equity portfolio to be down -26% (if marked-to-market).

Blindly following a return target, while it becomes increasingly difficult to reach, is perhaps irresponsible when you have no choice but to increase allocations to one of the riskiest asset classes in your portfolio.

This amplification of risk, especially into the second-longest economic expansion on record [8], may turn out fine, or it may not. What's an allocator to do? If the returns aren't there, then one cannot force it. Levering up is not the answer. Allocators should employ risk targeting, not return targeting. Allocate capital based on risk metrics, based on the organization's risk tolerance.

If one continues to use a constant return target, and not adjust it to a reasonable level based on risk tolerance and treasury yields, then one risks being caught swimming naked when the tide goes out during the next bear market. Don't let it be you.

---

[8] "Economic growth second-longest expansion on record," UNC Charlotte, 2019, https://inside.uncc.edu/news-features/2019-03-14/economic-growth-second-longest-expansion-record

6

The Ephemeral Nature of Stock Market Timing Signals

No stock market indicator is perfect. However, they are worthwhile to pay attention to. Take note of what they say and proceed with caution.

Stock market timing strategies have been around since the dawn of markets. They are utilized to forecast trends, from bear markets to bull markets, and everything in between. The goal in using stock market indicators is to be fully invested in bull markets and to side-step the drawdowns during bear markets.

The problem with stock market indicators is that if they worked reliably, then every market participant would use them. In a pari mutuel system such as the stock market, in which the dynamic pricing of the stock market changes the odds as people trade, the mere act of all participants utilizing the same forecasting system would render it useless.

With this in mind, let's take a look at a number of stock market indicators that have been used in the past.

Dividend Yields vs. Bond Yields

Between 1928 and 1958, the S&P 500 consistently yielded more than the 10-year Treasury bond, typically 2%-5% more. At this time, it was expected that ownership of common stocks was risky and a yield greater than government bonds was necessary to entice investors to go out on the risk curve and buy equities instead of treasuries.

When dividend yields were higher than bonds, own stocks. When bond yields exceeded dividend yields, own bonds.

In 1958, the yield on the 10-year bond exceeded that of the S&P 500 for the first time on record. Some investors would have taken this as a market timing signal to get out of stocks and put their capital into bonds, waiting for the market to "normalize", in which the yield on stocks would once again exceed the yield on bonds, to jump back into stocks.

But any investor relying on this stock and bond yield market timing strategy would have been waiting a *long* time, given that it took about 50 years for the 10-year bond yield to once again dip below the dividend yield of the S&P 500.

Obviously staying out of stocks for the period from 1958 to 2012 would have been a poor decision, making this stock market indicator unreliable.

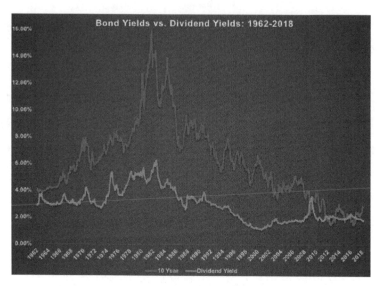

Source: Bloomberg[9]

The Buffett Indicator

The Buffett indicator compares the total market capitalization of U.S. stocks, as measured by the Wilshire 5000, to U.S. GDP.

This ratio compares the total value of publicly traded stocks to the country's economic output, with the theory that there should be a relationship between the two. When stocks are valued at a small portion of economic output, own stocks as

[9] Carlson, Ben. "Be Wary of the Gap Between Stock and Bond Yields," Bloomberg Opinion, 2018, https://www.bloomberg.com/opinion/articles/2018-03-07/be-wary-of-the-gap-between-stock-and-bond-yields

they are cheap. When stocks are valued at a large portion of economic output, do not own stocks as they are expensive.

Warren Buffett used this measure often, claiming "it is probably the best single measure of where valuations stand at any given moment". His key market cap / GDP rule, as discussed in a 2001 Fortune article [10], is:

"If the percentage relationship falls to the 70% or 80% area, buying stocks is likely to work very well for you. If the ratio approaches 200%--as it did in 1999 and a part of 2000--you are playing with fire."
-Warren Buffett

Buffett shut down his initial investment partnership in 1969, once the market cap / GDP indicator exceeded 80% for the first time.

The ratio came down significantly through the brutal bear market in the early 1970's and remained below the 80% threshold until 1995.

---

[10] Buffett & Loomis. "Warren Buffett on The Stock Market," Fortune, 2001,
https://archive.fortune.com/magazines/fortune/fortune_archive/2001/12/10/314691/index.htm

However, once the market cap / GDP indicator again crossed 80% in 1995, it never looked back. If investors would have taken this signal to sell stocks, as Buffett did in 1969, they would have been out of equities over the past 24 years, missing out the 700%+ total return of the S&P 500 over that time period. Note that Buffett's Berkshire Hathaway remained *very* invested in stocks over this period, ignoring his indicator for a gain of almost 1,200%.

For this signal to once again drop below 80% and prompt investors to stampede back into stocks, the equity index would have to drop -42% from its current level. Certainly, within the realm of possibilities, but I wouldn't hold your breath.

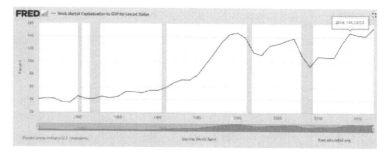

Source: Federal Reserve Bank of St. Louis [11]

---

[11] "Stock Market Capitalization to GDP for United States," FRED Economic Data, 2018, https://fred.stlouisfed.org/series/DDDM01USA156NWDB

CAPE

The cyclically adjusted price to earnings ratio (CAPE) is a valuation measure that averages real earnings per share over a 10-year period to generate a smoother, long-term earnings profile.

Prior to 1995, the CAPE ratio averaged 15x, oscillating around this mean with a low of 5x in 1921 and a high of nearly 35x in 1929.

The CAPE ratio crossed the 15x pre-1995 long-term average in 1995 and didn't subsequently cross below that mark save for a brief moment during the depths of the global financial crisis in 2008-2009.

The CAPE ratio is another stock market indicator that would have largely kept investors out of the market since 1995.

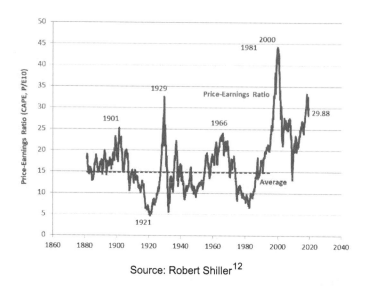

Source: Robert Shiller[12]

On a personal note, in 2011, the CAPE ratio crossed 23x to the upside, a level exceeded only during 1929 and the tech bubble of 1999-2000. I was concerned that valuations were stretched, as the market had rallied hard for a number of years coming out of the great recession and bear market of 2008.

Given these stretched valuations, I thought the timing was right to launch an event-driven arbitrage fund, a hedge fund strategy that can perform well irrespective of stock market performance. It was a strategy that I felt could generate positive performance even if the markets declined.

---

[12] "Online Data Robert Shiller," Yale, N.D., http://www.econ.yale.edu/~shiller/data.htm

I launched this strategy in January 2012 and over the subsequent years, my concern regarding stock valuations turned out to be unfounded. The markets continued to rally over the next seven years. Not only did the CAPE ratio not decline, it actually went up an additional 32%. The CAPE ratio currently sits at 30x; double the pre-1995 average.

Baltic Dry Index

During the global financial crisis of 2008-2009, one key leading economic indicator that emerged was the Baltic Dry Index (BDI).

The BDI is a composite of freight shipping rates and is regarded as a general shipping market bellwether. It was thought to provide insight into where the global economy was heading.

From 2006 to 2008, the BDI rallied alongside global markets. When the global financial crisis struck and stock markets globally dropped, the BDI also plunged.

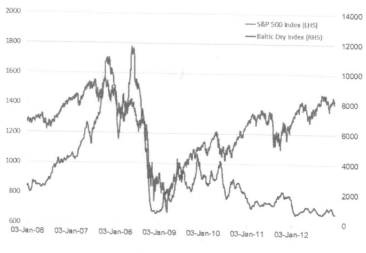

Source: Bloomberg

After both the BDI and stock markets recovered markedly in 2009, the BDI began showing weakness in 2010. Was this leading indicator correct in telling investors that the stock market was heading for a decline?

Nope. Turns out the BDI stopped working that year due to a deluge of ships being delivered, decimating shipping prices, and dragging the shipping index to new lows over the next nine years.

10-Year Minus 3-Month Yield Curve

The yield curve, measured as the difference between 10-year treasury bond yields and 3-month treasury bond yields,

44

is an indicator that many market participants have their eyes on these days as it recently hit a key level.

In a well-functioning market, the yield spread is typically 1%-3%, reflecting the spread that investors need to compensate them for the risk of holding longer tenor bonds.

It is only when the yield curve *inverts*, or when long-term 10-year yields drop below that of short-term 3-month yields, do warning bells start to ring. The yield curve just inverted for the first time since 2007.

The reason that a yield curve inversion is meaningful is that this indicator preceded all nine U.S. recessions since the 1950's, save for one false positive in 1966. Its track record in predicting recessions has been quite good over the past 65 years.

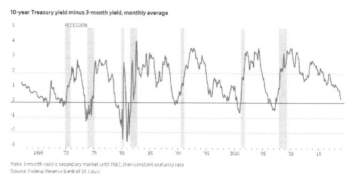

Source: Wall Street Journal [13]

Recessions typically beget significant stock market declines and many investors try to utilize a yield curve inversion to lessen up their stock market exposure in order to side-step any subsequent declines.

One note is on timing - the inverted yield curve doesn't have a great track record of indicating *when* a recession will commence. Historically, the yield curve has inverted anywhere from seven months to 24 months prior to a recession starting.

---

[13] Makintosh, James. "Inverted Yield Curve Is Telling Investors What They Already Know," The Wall Street Journal, 2019, https://www.wsj.com/articles/inverted-yield-curve-is-telling-investors-what-they-already-know-11553425200?mod=djemMoneyBeat_us&ns=prod/accounts-wsj

What To Do About It

Stock market history is filled with leading indicators, most of which have a spotty track record. Investors and traders have long relied on many of these to try to make short-term forecasts, with mixed results.

The recent inversion of the yield curve is a yellow flag for investors. Rather than exit all of your stocks, which has its downsides (taxes, timing, missed opportunities, etc.), investors should get comfortable with their asset allocation, the risk in their portfolio, and the potential downside should a bear market hit. Remember that recessions and drawdowns historically have been temporary and markets typically recoup their losses on their way to all-time highs, albeit sometimes after long periods, so a long-term mindset is imperative.

No stock market indicator is perfect. However, they are worthwhile to pay attention to. Take note of what they say and proceed with caution.

7

Merger Arbitrage: A Strategy for Consistent Profits in the Market

---

Merger arbitrage can represent an attractive allocation within a well-diversified investment portfolio given its absolute-return nature, low-risk profile, and low correlation to traditional asset classes.

Arbitrage is defined as the simultaneous buying and selling of an asset, such as a product or a stock, in different markets or in different forms to capitalize on the difference, or "spread" between the price one can buy and the price one can sell the same asset.

For example, many DIYers engage in retail arbitrage. An example is buying a microwave at the local Walmart for $50.00 and then selling it on Amazon.com for $55.00. The arbitrageur would pocket a $5.00 (10%) profit.

There are many different types of arbitrages in the capital markets, including currency arbitrage, interlisted arbitrage, convertible bond arbitrage, etc. One tried and true arbitrage trading strategy with a storied history involves the generation of arbitrage profits from announced mergers and acquisitions, known as merger arbitrage.

> "Give a man a fish and you will feed him for a day.
> Teach a man to arbitrage and you will feed him forever"
> – Warren Buffett

A Primer On Merger Arbitrage

When a company (the acquiror) seeks to acquire another company (the target), it typically needs to pay a premium over the target's unaffected share price. This premium is necessary because a target company's board of directors is only likely to recommend the acquisition of the company if the acquisition price is sufficiently higher than the current share price, otherwise the risk and effort of a deal aren't worthwhile.

[handwritten margin note: capitalizes on the spread]

Merger arbitrage is an investment strategy that capitalizes on the spread between a company's current share price and the consideration paid for its acquisition in the context of an announced merger transaction. The merger arbitrageur seeks to profit from buying, or going long, a takeover stock at a discount to its acquisition price.

[handwritten margin note: Buyers or sellers coming to buy at a discount to the acquisition price]

For a typical acquisition, an acquiror offers cash, shares, or a combination of both, to the target's shareholders. In the case where the merger consideration includes shares, the arbitrageur goes long the target stock (while) shorting the acquiror's stock at a ratio equivalent to the share consideration offered. While the share-based merger consideration's dollar value changes as the acquiror's share price changes, the arbitrageur "locks-in" the spread by

51

[handwritten note: Locks in the Acquiror's stock]

shorting the acquiror's stock to match the consideration offered. Whether the consideration includes cash or shares, the spread is earned once the deal closes successfully.

This spread between the acquisition price and the trading price of a stock exists to compensate the arbitrageur for the risk of the acquisition failing to close. If a deal falls apart, the arbitrageur typically suffers significant losses as the target shares fall precipitously to a price that no longer reflects a takeover premium.

The example below of IBM acquiring Red Hat details how a successful merger arbitrage trade works.

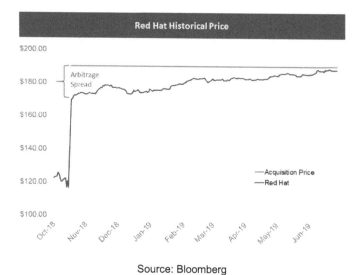

Source: Bloomberg

On October 28, 2018, technology company IBM announced the friendly acquisition of software provider Red Hat [14] for the consideration of $190.00 cash per Red Hat share. This $190.00 takeover price represented a 62.8% premium over Red Hat's unaffected closing price of $116.68 the day before the transaction was announced.

The companies indicated that they expected the deal to close "in the latter half of 2019". The transaction was subject to the approval of Red Hat shareholders, regulatory approvals, and other customary closing conditions.

Once the deal was publicly announced, Red Hat shares rocketed from $116.68 to $169.63, still markedly below the $190.00 announced price in which IBM would acquire Red Hat shares once the deal closed. Therein lies the opportunity for the merger arbitrageur. On that day, there was a $20.37, or 12.0%, spread between the trading price of Red Hat shares and the $190.00 acquisition price. This arbitrage spread, represented by the gap between the blue line of Red Hat's share price and the orange line of the acquisition price in the above chart, shrunk over time as the deal progressed and conditions to closing were satisfied. As

---

[14] IBM. "IBM To Acquire Red Hat, Completely Changing the Cloud Landscape And Becoming World's #1 Hybrid Cloud Provider," IBM Newsroom, 2018, https://newsroom.ibm.com/2018-10-28-IBM-To-Acquire-Red-Hat-Completely-Changing-The-Cloud-Landscape-And-Becoming-Worlds-1-Hybrid-Cloud-Provider

various deal conditions are met, the acquisition is de-risked, and this change in probabilities in the deal's chance of closing gets reflected in the target's share price as it meanders closer to the acquisition price.

For IBM's acquisition of Red Hat, using the actual closing date of July 9, 2019 (the companies guided to a "latter half of 2019" closing), the 12.0% merger arbitrage spread available in Red Hat shares equated to a 17.8% annualized return over the next 253 days.

A 17.8% annualized return is certainly very attractive, especially in an environment of rock-bottom yields. But that annualized return comes with a risk. If the deal falls apart, Red Hat shares would likely fall back down to the level where they were before the deal was announced, or about $116.00. On the first day, the merger arbitrageur is buying at $169.63 with the premise that the deal will close at a later date at $190.00, and if it fails, the stock would fall back down to around $116.68, where the stock was prior to the announcement of the deal. Therefore, the arbitrageur is risking $52.95 of downside to earn $20.37 of upside. This equates to a market-implied probability of the acquisition successfully closing at 72%.

The following equations lay out the calculation of upside, downside and probability of success in the Red Hat merger arbitrage:

Upside = Acquisition Price - Current Share Price = $190.00 - $169.63 = $20.37

Downside = Current Share Price - Unaffected Share Price = $169.63 - $116.68 = $52.95

Probability of Success = Downside / (Upside + Downside) = $52.95 / ($20.37 + $52.95) = 72%

There are many reasons why a deal can fall apart, including:
- Shareholders vote against deal;
- Regulators block deal;
- Financing falls through;
- Deterioration in company performance; and,
- Declining stock market causing the buyer to get cold feet.

A merger arbitrageur must be compensated for providing investors liquidity upon deal announcement. This compensation, in the form of the merger spread, is payment to the arbitrageurs for stepping in and providing the option

go long

for long-term shareholders to exit their stake quickly and not have to wait months for the deal to close.

On the first day of trading after the announcement of the IBM / Red Hat deal, the market implied probability of the deal closing was 72%. An arbitrageur would go long the Red Hat merger arbitrage if the deal had a greater than 72% probability of closing.

The deal did end up closing successfully on July 9, 2019, providing an attractive 17.8% annualized return to the arbitrageur.

Historical Returns From Merger Arbitrage

Merger arbitrage came to the forefront of hedge fund investment strategies during the takeover boom of the 1980's. When the strategy was still new and lacked substantial competition, returns were very high, with some arbitrage firms averaging returns above 20% per annum. Notably, Warren Buffett earned a 53% rate of return from his merger arbitrage investments in 1988. [15] These high returns

---

[15] Norris, Floyd. "Market Place; An Expert Shuns Risk Arbitrage" The New York Times, 1989,
https://www.nytimes.com/1989/03/28/business/market-place-an-expert-shuns-risk-
arbitrage.html?mtrref=www.google.com&gwh=B71258B249C3D29F398
0A93F9BBE4F6B&gwt=pay

were especially noteworthy given they generally weren't dependent on the direction of stock market indices. Merger arbitrage typically generates absolute returns - that is, positive investment returns irrespective of general stock market direction.

As with any successful investment strategy, the chance to attain these eye-popping returns attracted significant competition, compressing the returns available.

Over the years, as the strategy became more institutionalized and capital came looking to harvest merger arbitrage spreads, returns came down to a more pedestrian single-digit annualized return.

Over the past 15 years, merger arbitrage has been competitive with bonds, with the Eurekahedge Arbitrage Index beating the Bloomberg Barclays Aggregate Bond Index by about 0.5% per year, albeit with higher volatility.

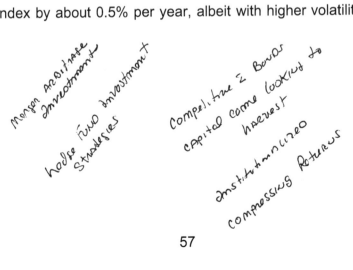

Merger Arbitrage Investment

Hedge fund Investment strategies

Competitive Bonds

Capital came looking to harvest

Institutionalized

compressing Returns

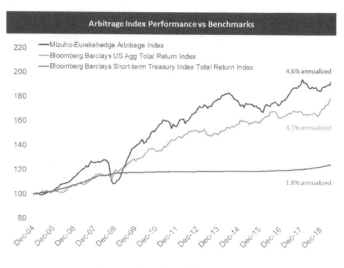

Source: Bloomberg, Eurekahedge

Merger Arbitrage As An Investment Strategy

The goal of a merger arbitrage strategy is to put together a diversified portfolio of arbitrage trades where each trade offers these three features:

1. Attractive annualized return above one's cost of capital;
2. Market-implied probability of success below one's estimate; and,
3. Idiosyncratic return expectation with low correlation to other trades.

The market sets the spread of each merger arbitrage opportunity based off of the risk-free rate, typically three-month treasuries, plus a risk premium. Since 2005, this risk premium has averaged about 3.0%. This is useful in setting expectations, with the current risk-free rate around 2.0%, average merger arbitrage returns are expected to be around 5.0% per year.

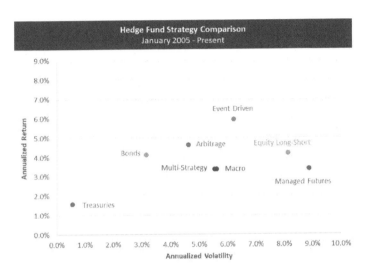

Source: Bloomberg, Eurekahedge

On average, merger arbitrage has outperformed most other hedge fund strategies on an absolute and risk-adjusted basis.

Cost of Capital

Risk Free Profit

Risk Free Rate

Risk Premium

Year	Mizuho-Eurekahedge Arbitrage Index	Bloomberg Barclays Short-term Treasury Index Total Return Index	Bloomberg Barclays US Agg Total Return Index
2005	2.6%	2.8%	2.4%
2006	11.2%	4.6%	4.3%
2007	10.6%	5.5%	7.0%
2008	-13.5%	3.4%	5.2%
2009	28.1%	0.6%	5.9%
2010	10.2%	0.4%	6.5%
2011	1.3%	0.3%	7.8%
2012	9.0%	0.2%	4.2%
2013	5.2%	0.2%	-2.0%
2014	-1.9%	0.1%	6.0%
2015	-2.3%	0.1%	0.5%
2016	2.0%	0.6%	2.6%
2017	9.0%	0.8%	3.5%
2018	-2.6%	1.9%	0.0%
YTD 2019	4.0%	1.5%	6.1%
Annualized Return	**4.6%**	**1.6%**	**4.1%**

Source: Bloomberg

While merger arbitrage has historically exhibited low correlation to both treasuries and the broad-based bond index, it has provided similar low volatility returns to these fixed income strategies and the returns were positive most years. Given this characteristic, merger arbitrage can be thought of as an alternative to fixed income.

However, there are a few main advantages of merger arbitrage compared to bonds:

- Merger arbitrage returns are driven off of a risk spread based on short-term treasuries. Therefore, merger spreads don't take duration risk given the trades' short tenor and can be thought of similarly to a floating-rate yield.

- Merger arbitrage returns typically consist of capital gains and therefore are taxed more efficiently than the income produced by bonds.

What's Worse Than Heartbreak? Deal Break

So far, we have outlined that merger arbitrage can provide attractive, consistent low-risk returns over time. Where can the strategy go wrong?

A broken deal can be very costly for an arbitrageur. When an acquisition falls apart, losses suffered can be 10x, or higher, than the expected profit from a successful arbitrage investment. Given an arbitrageur typically needs 10 successful arbitrage trades to make up for a broken deal, the strategy should be conducted within a robust risk-management framework. Diversification is key.

Luckily, there exists an upside scenario in an arbitrage trade - the bidding war.

A bidding war occurs when an interloper unexpectedly offers a higher price for the target company. In this situation, the arbitrageur will profit well in excess of the original expected spread as the acquisition price offered either by the interloper, or the increased bid offered by the original acquiror, tends to be materially higher than the starting bid. One lucrative bidding war for a target can make an investor's year.

The below pie chart displays the outcome of all mergers and acquisitions in Canada from 2010 to 2018.

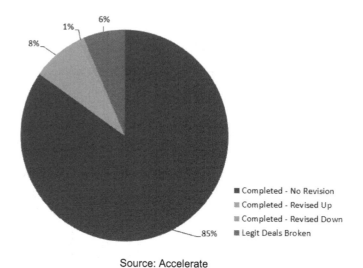

Source: Accelerate

Historically, 94% of announced mergers have closed, with 85% closing at the initial deal terms, 8% with higher deal terms, and 1% with lower deal terms. As for deals falling apart, 6% of announced transactions have failed to close.

The Arbitrage Playbook

Given the assumption that 94% of deals close successfully, the goal of the arbitrageur is to put together a diversified portfolio of arbitrage investments that reflect an average market-implied probability of closing less than 94%.

For example, generally the merger arbitrage market prices the average probability of closing, throughout the entire deal universe, at around 85%. This reflects the inherent return for the arbitrageur - the average implied probability of the successful closing of a portfolio of arbitrage investments of 85% compared to the historical average closing rate of 94% that represents the mispricing of odds in the arbitrageur's favor. Harvesting this mispricing with a diversified portfolio of arbitrage investments can produce an attractive return over time.

Feeding Forever Off Arbitrage

Merger arbitrage can represent an attractive allocation within a well-diversified investment portfolio given its absolute-return nature, low-risk profile, and low correlation to traditional asset classes. However, given the resource and time-intensive nature of the strategy, along with the need to have a well-diversified portfolio of arbitrage

63

investments, individual investors who cannot dedicate themselves full-time to the strategy should steer clear of merger arbitrage and seek to allocate to an arbitrage fund run by a professional.

Warren Buffett said, "teach a man to arbitrage and you will feed him forever," meaning arbitrage is an essential investment strategy that aims to generate consistent results in the future. And investors need to eat.

8

The Myth of the Illiquidity Premium

Self-inflicted illiquidity does not magically create the illiquidity premium.

Private equity firms are known to charge some of the highest fees in the investment management business. Accounting for management fees and performance fees (also known as "carry"), the management expense ratio of the average private equity fund is around 5% per year. In this competitive environment, a 5% annual fee to manage funds seems excessive and difficult to justify.

Empirical research [16] shows that historically private equity fund returns have been driven by three quantitative factors:

- Value Factor - buying cheaper stocks has historically outperformed;
- Size Factor - buying shares of smaller companies has historically outperformed; and,
- Leverage - using copious amounts of debt magnifies returns.

These three factors are relatively easy to replicate. Private equity funds have been charging high fees for returns that are somewhat commoditized. In order to justify these high fees beyond the simple three factors driving their returns, they need to point to something less tangible and more mysterious and complicated. This is an "illiquidity premium,"

---

[16] Stafford, Erik. "Replicating Private Equity with Value Investing, Homemade Leverage, and Hold-to-Maturity Accounting." Harvard Business School Working Paper, No. 16-081, January 2016.

which is the mysterious factor that many leveraged buyout firms claim produces outsized returns.

This illiquidity premium is a thing - what it means is that you earn higher returns for an illiquid (i.e., difficult to sell) investment. Let's consider an example. Say you can open a savings account that you can withdraw anytime, and it offers a 3% interest rate. The second savings account option can only be withdrawn after five years. All else being equal, what interest rate would you require from the second account in which you're unable to get your money back for five years? Certainly, higher than the first account's 3% interest rate. The higher interest rate above 3% needed for the second "illiquid" account is called the illiquidity premium.

The key to understanding the illiquidity premium is that it comes from somewhere - the discount you pay for an investment given you won't be able to sell it for a while. It is from this discount in which the illiquidity premium is earned.

The problem with traditional private equity (aka leveraged buyouts) is that it typically buys an investment from a liquid public market and takes it private, where it then becomes illiquid. This "self-inflicted" illiquidity does not magically create the illiquidity premium. As we know, the illiquidity premium comes from buying an illiquid asset at a discount

67

compared to the price of its liquid brethren. This is where the private equity scheme falls apart. Not only do they not buy the assets at a discount, but they pay what's called a "control premium", which is typically around 30% higher than the liquid market price.

Let's take a look at another example. Say ABC Corp trades in the stock market at $10.00 per share. Over the next five years, the value of the business increases by 50% and the stock is now worth 50% more, or $15.00 per share.

Say Private Equity LP wants to take over ABC Corp when it is trading at $10.00 per share. Private Equity LP will need to pay a control premium, so let's say it pays $13.00 per share (a 30% control premium). Five years down the line, ABC Corp's business increases the same amount and it now has a market value of $15.00 per share. Remember, Private Equity LP has taken ABC Corp private in this scenario and therefore it is illiquid.

So, the return for ABC Corp over the five years is 50% (stock appreciates from $10.00 to $15.00), but the return for Private Equity LP is only about 15% (it paid $13.00 for it and it was worth $15.00 five years later), excluding the 5% per year fee.

So, the illiquid investment owner by Private Equity LP earned a far lower return than the liquid investment.

This shows that not only is there no illiquidity premium attained in this example, as one cannot self-administer this premium, there is actually a large drag on investment returns for Private Equity LP from the control premium it needs to pay.

The illiquidity premium in leveraged buyouts is a myth perpetuated by private equity firms to justify their high fees. But where do their returns come from? In addition to the value and size factors, the magic of private equity returns comes from... LEVERAGE (or debt as most people call it). They are called leveraged buyout firms for a reason.

9

Replicating Private Equity with Liquid Public Securities

The returns of leveraged buyouts come from three investment factors: value, size, and leverage. Private equity performance can be replicated.

Fundraising for the private equity industry has been knocking it out of the park over the past number of years, with $3 trillion raised from investors since 2012.[17] As one private equity firm remains on track to raise the largest leveraged buyout fund in history, 2019 is set to break records as the biggest yet for fundraising. In fact, the demand for private equity from institutional investors is so insatiable that the industry has over $1.2 trillion of "dry powder,"[18] a substantial amount of capital in excess of the current investable opportunity set.

Funds Moving From Medium-Fee To High-Fee

The continued rise in private equity commitments from investors lays in stark contrast to fund flows in active long-only public equities, which continue to suffer massive net outflows. Nearly $1 trillion[19] has been redeemed from active mutual funds over the past four years.

---

[17] Franklin & Manjesh. "Blackstone buyout fund raises $22 billion, to set record: source," Journal Pioneer, 2019, https://www.journalpioneer.com/business/business/blackstone-buyout-fund-raises-22-billion-to-set-record-source-297530/

[18] McCabe, Carrie. "Not Enough Private Equity to Go Around," Forbes, 2019, https://www.forbes.com/sites/carriemccabe/2019/03/28/not-enough-private-equity-to-go-around/#41ab515371ad

[19] Balchunas, Eric. "A Bear Market Would Be a Death Knell for Active Funds," Bloomberg Opinion, 2018, https://www.bloomberg.com/opinion/articles/2018-05-03/a-bear-market-would-be-a-death-knell-for-active-funds

This dichotomy between long-only active public investing and long-only active private investing is especially perplexing given the trend of allocators moving from high-cost active strategies to low-cost passive strategies. Private equity has some of the highest fees in the investment management business, estimated at[20] 6%-7% per year. Notably, some private equity firms have been increasing their performance fees from 20%-30%, while active mutual fund and hedge fund fees continue to be pressured to the downside.

Systematic Firms Seek To Disrupt Private Equity

Given the bounty of fees of private equity, it's no surprise that systematic funds have developed strategies to disrupt the private equity model by replicating its returns through systematic strategies. These quantitative private equity replication strategies are now coming to the forefront.

According to a Harvard Business School study,[21] it is possible to replicate private equity returns with liquid public

---

[20] Doskeland & Stromberg. "Evaluating Investments in Unlisted Equity for The Norwegian Government Pension Fund Global (Gpfg)." Stockholm School of Economics, 2018, https://www.regjeringen.no/contentassets/7fb88d969ba34ea6a0cd9225b28711a9/evaluating_doskelandstromberg_10012018.pdf

[21] Stafford, Erik. "Replicating Private Equity with Value Investing, Homemade Leverage, and Hold-to-Maturity Accounting," Harvard Business School, 2015,

securities. "A passive portfolio of small, low EBITDA (earnings before interest, taxes, depreciation, and amortization - a commonly used measure of cash flow) multiple stocks with modest amounts of leverage and hold-to-maturity accounting of net asset value produces an unconditional return distribution that is highly consistent with that of the pre-fee aggregate private equity index."

We believe that Harvard has it right, despite claims from private equity executives insisting otherwise. Private equity firms typically insist that their market-beating investment performance comes from the "illiquidity premium", along with operational improvements at their portfolio companies.

We have already dispelled the misconception that leveraged buyouts earn any illiquidity premium:

> *"The key to understanding the illiquidity premium is that it comes from somewhere – the discount you pay for an investment given you won't be able to sell it for a while. It is from this discount in which the illiquidity premium is earned.*

https://www.hbs.edu/faculty/Publication%20Files/ReplicatingPE_201512_3859877f-bd53-4d3e-99aa-6daec2a3a2d3.pdf

The problem with traditional private equity (aka leveraged buyouts) is that they typically buy an investment from a liquid public market and take it private, where it then becomes illiquid. This self-inflicted illiquidity does not magically create the illiquidity premium. As we know, the illiquidity premium comes from buying an illiquid asset at a discount compared to the price of its liquid brethren. This is where the private equity scheme falls apart. Not only do they not buy the assets at a discount, but they pay what's called a control premium, which is typically around 30% higher than the liquid market price."

- The Myth of The Illiquidity Premium [22]

The assertion of substantial operating improvements at private equity portfolio companies is also a dubious claim. When a company goes private in a leveraged buyout, it does so by taking on a significant amount of debt. This dramatic increase in debt results in a significantly larger portion of its operating cash flow needed to cover interest payments and debt amortization, reducing capital available for growth initiatives. In addition, many private equity firms seek to pursue a dividend recapitalization as quickly as possible

---

[22] Klymochko, Julian. "The Myth of Illiquidity Premium," Accelerate, 2019, https://accelerateshares.com/blog/the-myth-of-the-illiquidity-premium/

after a go-private transaction, in which they look to dividend out any available cash from a portfolio company to themselves in a bid to recoup their cost base quickly. Not to mention that most publicly traded firms are well aware of the common financial engineering techniques that generate shareholder value, and likely have executed on these initiatives well before private equity shows up.

A study of leveraged buyouts revealed that earnings after two years under private equity ownership came in more than 33% below forecasts, according to S&P[23]. The notion of operating improvements at private equity portfolio companies is just a smokescreen used for marketing purposes.

Replicating Private Equity

Using the tenets derived from the Harvard Business School study, a systematic multifactor model can be crafted to replicate private equity returns using liquid public securities. This private equity multifactor model is driven by three main factors:

---

[23] Smith, Eric. "Equivalent of doping? Private equity takes juicing the numbers to the next level," Financial Times, 2019, https://www.ft.com/content/faa4406e-5f6c-11e9-b285-3acd5d43599e

76

1. **Size** - Select a universe of small- and mid-cap stocks. Why? Because small- and mid-cap stocks have historically outperformed.

2. **Value** - Select top decile value stocks on EBITDA-to-EV (the ratio of earnings before interest, taxes, depreciation, and amortization to enterprise value). Why? Because historically low valuation stocks have outperformed.

3. **Leverage** - Apply a modest amount of leverage to the portfolio. Why? Because leverage amplifies returns.

Below we run a simulation featuring North American small- and mid-cap stocks in the top decile EBITDA-to-EV value factor. This monthly-rebalanced, gross-of-fees (but net of trading expenses) Private Equity Replication portfolio is displayed in the following graph.

77

Source: Preqin, Compustat, S&P Capital IQ

The Private Equity Replication portfolio returned 144%, or 8.8% annualized. The Preqin Buyout Index, which aggregates private equity fund returns on a quarterly basis, returned 166%, or 9.5% annualized.

Despite similar performance of the Preqin Buyout Index and the Private Equity Replication portfolio, there are some distinct differences between the two underlying portfolios, which make the Preqin Buyout Index return profile somewhat difficult to believe.

For example, the average leverage, or debt level, for leveraged buyouts [24] in 2018 was 6.4x EBITDA. In contrast, the most recent leverage metric for the Private Equity Replication portfolio was only 1.1x EBITDA, with the most levered stock in the portfolio at 5.4x net debt / EBITDA (far lower than even the private equity average).

Somehow, the Preqin Buyout Index exhibits a fraction of the volatility of the Private Equity Replication portfolio, yet it is leveraged nearly 6x higher! This must be magic right? Perhaps it is, however, this is not the traditional magic of wizards and magicians, but the financial magic of mark-to-model accountants and analysts. Mark-to-model refers to the fact that private equity firms themselves determine the quarterly valuations of their portfolio holdings. They make sure to keep their investments out of the purview of the notoriously fickle public markets. Instead of accepting the marks of the collective market, consisting of thousands of analysts and computer algorithms coming to consensus on the price of an investment, private equity firms are blissfully free to mark their holdings to their view of "fair value" on a quarterly basis. Unsurprisingly, one firm's view of its investment value no doubt is almost always higher than it

---

[24] Gottfried, Miriam. "LBO Volume Surges as KKR, Others Put $1 Trillion Cash Pile to Work," The Wall Street Journal, 2018, https://www.wsj.com/articles/lbo-volume-surges-as-kkr-others-put-1-trillion-cash-pile-to-work-1528887600

was last quarter. This is important, because any decrease in valuation can lead to devastating unrealized losses for the private equity firms, due to the high leverage and its magnifying effects on performance.

A cardinal rule of investing dictates that the higher the leverage, the higher the volatility, and private equity portfolio companies push leverage to the max. Even mark-to-model accounting can't dispute that. Clearly, private equity volatility (and lack thereof) is pure fantasy. The net result of mark-to-model accounting is a material understating of risk in the portfolio. But not all investors believe the low-volatility fallacy of private equity marketing materials. One of the largest investors[25] in private equity funds even assumes that leveraged buyouts are over 30% more volatile than public equities.

If we add more leverage to the Private Equity Replication portfolio and utilize a more manager-friendly, quarterly mark-to-market pricing methodology, then our Private Equity Replication portfolio looks even better than the Preqin Buyout Index. The Leveraged & Smoothed version of the Private Equity Replication portfolio ran 130% long and

---

[25] "The Yale Endowment," Yale University, 2018, https://static1.squarespace.com/static/55db7b87e4b0dca22fba2438/t/5c8b09008165f55d4bec1a36/1552615684090/2018+Yale+Endowment.pdf

hedged with a 30% short in the S&P 500 index, as shown in grey below. The smoothing comes from only marking-to-market once per quarter.

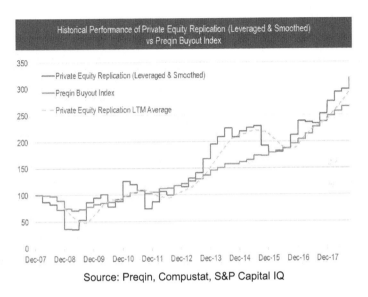

Source: Preqin, Compustat, S&P Capital IQ

Over the measurement period, the Leveraged Private Equity Replication portfolio returned 220%, or 11.4% annualized, vs. 166%, or 9.5% annualized from the Preqin Buyout Index.

Get The Benefits Of Private Equity By Losing Your Account Password

Private equity's market-beating returns generally do not come from the harvesting of the illiquidity premium, nor operational improvements at portfolio companies. The returns of leveraged buyouts come from three investment factors: value, size, and leverage. Private equity performance can be replicated with systematic strategies based on these three factors.

The more one reflects, the more one realizes that the main draw of private equity is the mark-to-model accounting, which leads to investors being unaware of true underlying portfolio risk. Certainly, a portfolio of small- and mid-cap stocks leveraged over 6x would exhibit some gut-wrenching volatility. Combine this with the inability to liquidate one's investment in a private equity fund when markets are stressed, and you have a great vehicle to harvest gains from leveraged small-cap value stocks by preventing investors from making mistakes by selling at the lows.

Is the lack of liquidity, which prevents investors from making poor investment decisions, worth paying a 6%-7% annual fee for? I'd recommend saving the fees, investing in a liquid private equity replication strategy and not checking your account for seven years. You'll likely end up with a better result at the end of it.

10

Playing Both Offense and Defense with Factor Investing

Factor strategies have the best chance of outperforming throughout various market environments with a balanced combination of both long and short portfolios.

Growing up on the Canadian prairies, like most kids, I played hockey. I was a left winger and had a penchant for scoring goals (what kid doesn't?). For what I lacked in size and skill, I tried to make up in cherry-picking ability. I figured I could maximize the expected amount of goals I'd score if I only played offense aggressively, and never back checked or played defensive hockey.

While this strategy helped my team put up goals, it certainly did not help prevent goals against. Thankfully, my line was stocked with talented defensemen who made up for my lack of defensive skills.

Like any competitive endeavour, the best strategies to win typically combine a balanced approach of both offensive and defensive play. Investing is no different.

Scoring With Factors

Factor investing, commonly known as "smart beta", is a rules-based style of investing in which portfolio securities are selected based on certain characteristics associated with higher returns.

These characteristics, known as factors, are persistent drivers of risk and return that can be systematically utilized to select securities to create portfolios that may outperform.

The Momentum Factor

For example, the momentum factor, applied to equity investing, involves buying winning stocks and shorting losing stocks. One implementation of the momentum factor is the 52-week high anomaly. This momentum strategy, detailed in George and Hwang's 2004 paper titled, "The 52-Week High and Momentum Investing," [26] involves going long stocks near their 52-week high while going short stocks far from their 52-week high.

Stocks near their 52-week highs outperform and stocks near their 52-week low underperform. In a nutshell, good stocks tend to continue to do well and bad stocks tend to continue to do poorly.

Running the 52-week high strategy on Canadian stocks over the past 20 years yields the following results:

---

[26] Thomas & Chuan-Yang. "The 52-Week High and Momentum Investing," The Journal of Finance, 2004, https://www.bauer.uh.edu/tgeorge/papers/gh4-paper.pdf

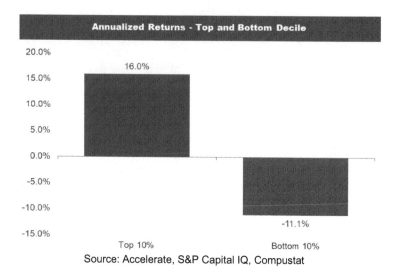

Source: Accelerate, S&P Capital IQ, Compustat

The top decile portfolio returned 16.0% per year, while the bottom decile portfolio returned -11.1% per year.

A $100,000 investment into the top decile portfolio, rebalanced on a monthly basis, results in a portfolio worth approximately $2 million after 20 years.

A $100,000 investment into the bottom decile portfolio, rebalanced on a monthly basis, results in a portfolio worth approximately $10,000 after 20 years (a -90% loss).

As you can see, the top decile portfolio massively outperforms while the bottom 10% portfolio significantly underperforms.

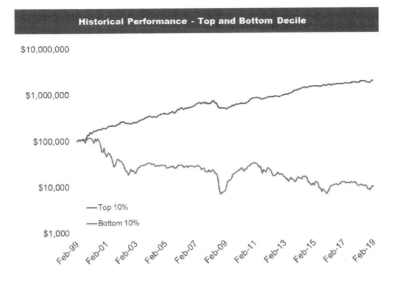

Source: Accelerate, S&P Capital IQ, Compustat

An enterprising investor can harvest the underperforming bottom decile portfolio by shorting it. This allows the investor not only to gain from the short portfolio, but also hedge out the market risk associated with the long portfolio and earn returns on a hedged basis.

Factor Investing: Hockey Stick Growth

Factor-based investment strategies can be readily programmed and implemented within an ETF. Factor strategies effectively quantify what many human portfolio management teams do, but use inexpensive computing power instead of teams of analysts and portfolio managers.

87

Because of this, factor strategies can be implemented cost-effectively.

Aside from the cost savings, historically, factor strategies have outperformed traditional actively managed mutual funds [27].

Given the potential cost savings and outperformance of factor strategies, it's no wonder asset growth has been robust. U.S. smart beta ETF strategies are expected to exceed $1 trillion in assets [28] by 2020.

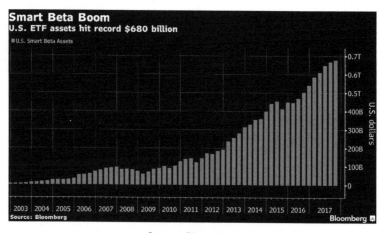

Source: Bloomberg

---

[27] Van Gelderen, Huij, & Kyosev. "Factor Investing from Concept to Implementation," SSRN, 2019,
https://papers.ssrn.com/sol3/papers.cfm?abstract_id=3313364
[28] Ang, Andrew. "Factors making waves," BlackRock, 2018,
https://www.blackrock.com/us/individual/investment-ideas/what-is-factor-investing/factor-commentary/andrews-angle/factor-growth

Smart Beta: A Half-Assed Implementation

Although used synonymously, smart beta, as implemented through ETFs, is not actually factor investing. True factor investing involves both going long the top quantile securities within that factor, while also going short the bottom quantile securities within said factor. This is done to produce true alpha, or outperformance. A robust factor should show the top quantile outperforming the mean, along with the bottom quantile underperforming the mean.

Smart beta ETFs are literally implementing factor strategies *half-assed*. They are implementing the long top quantile portion of the strategy, but leaving out the short bottom quantile and missing half the strategy, which misses half of the potential outperformance. They are all offense and no defense. The short portfolio tends to show strong gains when the market declines, which can help cushion losses from the long portion of the portfolio.

The Long And Short Of It

Academic research, which is where factor strategies are derived from, demonstrates that factor strategies have the best performance when executed using a long-short approach.

Much like a hockey team with a good combination of offense and defense, factor strategies have the best chance of outperforming throughout various market environments with a balanced combination of both long and short portfolios.

Don't be a cherry-picker. Play some defense.

11

Value Investing is Dead! #FAKENEWS

Don't believe the fake news. Value still works and the EV / EBITDA and EV / FCF metrics are still going strong.

Value investing's obituary has been written numerous times over the past decade. The reason attributed to its death is poor performance. Is this reality or is it fake news?

The Found Art Of Value Investing

Value investing, the practice of buying securities deemed undervalued compared to their intrinsic value, was brought to the forefront of investment management by Ben Graham with his seminal book, "Security Analysis", first published in 1934.

Typically, stocks are deemed to be of the "value" category if they are trading at a low multiple of a certain fundamental financial metric relative to the market multiple. For example, a stock may be undervalued based on various measures such as:

- book value;
- net earnings;
- free cash flow; or,
- EBITDA.

These metrics lead to valuation multiples such as:

- price to book value (P / B);
- price to earnings (P / E);
- enterprise value to free cash flow (EV / FCF); or,

- enterprise value to earnings before interest taxes depreciation and amortization (EV / EBITDA).

Value investing has been around for nearly 100 years. Graham practiced value investing in his investment partnership throughout the Great Depression, in which he focused on buying stocks trading for less than their net current asset value (NCAV). Graham defined the quantitative formula for buying shares of companies for substantially less than their NCAV, being the company's current assets less its total liabilities and preferred shares. Purchasing shares at this low valuation gave Graham what he deemed a "margin of safety". He viewed the NCAV as the value that a company could be liquidated, or sold for scrap for, and insisted on buying stocks trading below this level. NCAV is a balance sheet valuation metric similar to that of book value.

Graham had a number of well-known disciples who went on to have illustrious investment careers utilizing his strategy of buying securities trading below their intrinsic value.

Value Gains Momentum In Academic Circles

A few decades later, academic researchers began to study these value investing techniques. Specifically, in 1977, S.

Basu published a paper titled, "Investment Performance of Common Stocks in Relation to Their Price-Earnings Ratios: A Test Of The Efficient Market Hypothesis." This paper backtested a value strategy based on the P/E ratio, a common value metric, and found that "the low P/E portfolios seem to have on average, earned a higher absolute and risk-adjusted rates of return than the high P/E securities". According to Basu, value investing worked.

In 1992, Eugene Fama and Kenneth French popularized value investing with their paper "Common risk factors in the returns on stocks and bonds". This paper built off the findings of other studies completed throughout the 1980's. One factor that Fama and French popularized with their research was the book-to-market value factor, or the inverse of price-to-book value multiple.

This value factor, book-to-market, indicated that stocks at high book-to-market (i.e., low price compared to their book value) tend to outperform, while stocks at low book-to-market (i.e., high price compared to their book value) tend to underperform.

The Problem With Value

Many firms took the value factor and ran with it. The book-to-market value investing methodology proliferated within investment firms, as its noted outperformance obviously held mass appeal.

The book-to-market factor was so successful that now the top 15 value ETFs in the U.S., managing approximately $180 billion of assets, all use the book-to-market factor to some extent in their index methodologies (some based solely on book-to-market and some a composite of various value factors including book-to-market).

In fact, the most frequently pointed-to gauge of value investing's performance, the popular Russell Value Indexes, is solely built off of the book-to-market factor.

If you ever read an article about how value is outperforming or underperforming, it is almost always referring to one of the Russell Value Indexes.

The vast majority of value strategies and indexes are based on the book-to-market factor.

95

The problem here is straightforward: The book-to-market factor doesn't work. It sucks and is not a good measurement of value at all. Let me explain.

A company's book value used to be a decent proxy for its intrinsic value, but stopped working decades ago. If you ask fundamental investors to analyze and value a stock, rarely, if ever, will they look at book value. It just isn't meaningful anymore for a number of reasons. First, the accounting treatment of corporate actions, such as acquisitions and share buybacks, have made book value essentially meaningless. Second, the proliferation in the stock market of more asset-light, service-based businesses, which typically earn income from valuable intangible assets whose value, is not properly captured in a company's accounting measure of book value.

If book value is mostly meaningless these days, then what company metric can be used to appropriately measure a stock's valuation?

The answer lies in cash flow, or some variant thereof. My favourite methodologies are to compare Enterprise Value to EBITDA or free cash flow. Enterprise value is superior to that of just price, because it takes into account the entire firm value, including debt, equity and preferred stock, rather than just equity. Cash flow measures, such as EBITDA and FCF, are better than balance sheet measures, such as book value, as cash flow values a business based on a going-concern value while book value looks on a liquidation basis. Most public companies are more appropriately valued as a going-concern as opposed to a liquidation - they tend to be worth more alive than dead.

The Proof Is In The Pudding

A comparison of the simulated performance of a market neutral (100% long/ 100% short) strategy of all three value factors, book-to-market, FCF to EV, and EBITDA to EV, is shown below:

Comparative 20-Year Single-Factor Portfolio Performance Across Value Factors (Canada)

Source: Accelerate, S&P Capital IQ, Compustat

Starting 20 years ago, $1 million is invested in each value factor's long-short portfolio. These portfolios go long top decile and short bottom decile of the specific factor. This means they go long the most undervalued stocks, according to the value factor, and short the most overvalued stocks.

To make this simulation as realistic as we could, the simulations utilize a risk model and account for commissions, market impact, and short borrow fees. The portfolios are rebalanced monthly.

As you can see, over the 20-year time frame the FCF to EV and EBITDA to EV factors had outstanding performance, while the book-to-market factor had a rough go of it.

	Book to Market	FCF to EV	EBITDA to EV
Portfolio Value	$500,611	$5,356,171	$5,269,244
Cumulative Return	-50%	436%	427%
Annualized Return	-3.4%	8.8%	8.7%

The $1 million long-short portfolio in the FCF to EV and EBITDA to EV strategies would both be worth $5.3 million after 20 years, for a cumulative return of over 400% and nearly 9% annualized.

That same portfolio in the book-to-market strategy would have been halved to $0.5 million, for a cumulative return of -50%, or -3.4% annualized.

98

Value Investing Isn't Dead

As you can see, value investing isn't dead, however, book-to-market sure is. From a fundamental perspective, investing based off of a company's book value makes little sense. Historical simulations, along with underperformance of the Russel Value Indexes, prove this point.

Don't believe the fake news. Value still works and the EV / EBITDA and EV / FCF metrics are still going strong. Long live value investing!

12

Whatever You Do, Don't Invest Based on Dividend Yield

The main reason we're against investing based solely on dividends is that the dividend yield is not a robust factor; it is not predictive of excess future returns.

The classic thinking that many amateur investors, and even some professionals, have is that if you buy a stock with a high dividend yield, you should do well in the markets. Certainly, there is no shortage of dividend-investing hype and catch phrases:

"Income Investing!"

"Get Paid to Wait!"

Ever since the global financial crisis of 2008-2009 brought interest rates to rock-bottom levels, many investors have turned to buying dividend stocks to earn income. I mean, what could be so bad about collecting quarterly dividend cheques?

Turns out, focusing exclusively on dividends may be bad for your financial health.

Dividends Just Don't Matter Anymore

A corporation has five main areas to allocate capital:
1) Capital expenditures ("capex");
2) Research and development ("R&D");
3) Mergers and acquisitions ("M&A");
4) Dividends; and,

5) Share buybacks.

The first three choices, capex, R&D an M&A, stem from the company's decision to reinvest its free cash flow for growth initiatives.

Dividends and share buybacks, also known as "shareholder yield" when combined, are ways to return cash to shareholders. When a corporation produces excess free cash flow, it can return cash to shareholders either via dividends or share buybacks. From a corporation's perspective, both dividends and share buybacks are the same thing except that share buybacks are a more tax efficient method of returning capital to investors.

Throughout most of capital markets history, share buybacks were actually illegal. It wasn't until 1982, when the SEC passed a new rule allowing for buybacks, did the composition of shareholder yield begin to change.

Prior to the emergence of buybacks in 1982, dividends were important and were typically decent proxies for free cash flow of a corporation.

However, over the past few decades, there has been a bonanza in the growth of share buybacks. In the S&P 500

Index, buybacks have become so pervasive that the buyback yield is nearly 4%, or almost double the index's dividend yield. Buybacks now account for two-thirds of the S&P 500's shareholder yield of 6%.

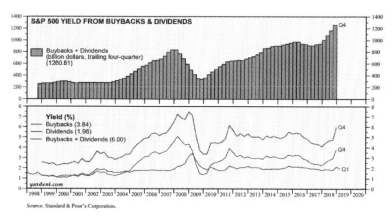

Source: Yardeni Research [29]

The S&P 500 buyback yield has exceeded its dividend yield almost every year since 2005. Therefore, it is more important to look at share buybacks when evaluating cash payments from corporations to shareholders, as buybacks now account for the lion's share of shareholder yield.

---

[29] Yardeni, Abbott, Quintana. "Stock Market Indicators: S&P 500 Buybacks & Dividends," Yardeni Research, 2019, https://www.yardeni.com/pub/buybackdiv.pdf

Easy To Manipulate

There's a dirty little secret that many income investors don't know:

Theoretically, a company can arbitrarily set its dividend yield, as long as it has access to cash, liquid assets or a line of credit. When a company pays out more money than it produces in free cash flow, it can fund this by partially self-liquidating to pay an artificially high dividend, at least temporarily.

Artificially high dividends are often seen in the closed-end fund space. Many closed-end funds (which shall remain nameless) set their dividend yields artificially high, typically north of a 10% yield, when the underlying portfolio only generates sub-5% dividend yields, in order to attract less sophisticated investors in search of yield. This dividend is mostly return of capital - effectively paying investors their money back as the closed-end fund slowly liquidates to fund the payments.

Artificially high dividends were once a popular business model for income trusts. Trusts used to pay distributions in excess of their free cash flow, making up the difference by regularly raising capital via equity issuance. However, raising money from new investors to pay old investors has a negative connotation to it (Ponzi), and this business model generally doesn't last very long.

Out of the investable universe of Canadian stocks (i.e., those trading above $2.00), 62% of stocks pay a dividend. However, 45% of Canadian stocks generated negative free cash flow over the past year. 19% of Canadian stocks paid a dividend while generating negative free cash flow and 34% of publicly traded Canadian companies paid a dividend last year that they couldn't cover with their positive free cash flow.

Don't Be Fooled By A Fat Dividend

An example of investors being drawn into an overvalued, underperforming stock based solely on its high dividend yield is the BP Prudhoe Bay Royalty Trust (BPT). This trust owns one asset, being a royalty from BP's Prudhoe Bay oilfield on the North Slope of Alaska. The trust pays a variable quarterly dividend based on the royalties it receives, which depend on oilfield production levels and the price of oil.

Given the depleting nature of the oilfield, BPT expects to stop receiving royalty payments after 2022.[30] Since dividends are expected to cease in three-and-a-half years, it's easy to discern that BPT is overvalued based on the present value of its expected future dividends, with the last quarterly dividend being $0.35 per share.

At the start of the year, BPT was yielding over 25% annualized, based on its Q4 dividend payment of $1.38 per share. Investors bid up the stock to a price far above intrinsic value, the present value of its future cash flows, based on this apparent juicy dividend yield.

However, reality struck when the trust announced the Q2 dividend of only $0.35 per share, which sent BPT shares tumbling -14%. Investors aware of BPT's intrinsic value, which is relatively easy to model, would have not owned the stock and therefore would have sidestepped the carnage. Investors owning the shares exclusively for the dividend would have been shellacked.

---

[30] "Morningstar® Document Research," Bp Prudhoe Bay Royalty Trust – Bpt, 2019,
http://app.quotemedia.com/data/downloadFiling?ref=12750962&type=PDF&symbol=BPT&companyName=BP+Prudhoe+Bay+Royalty+Trust&formType=10-K&formDescription=Annual+report+with+a+comprehensive+overview+of+the+company&dateFiled=2019-03-01

A Poor Man's Value And Quality Factors

The main reason we're against investing based solely on dividends is that the dividend yield is not a robust factor; it is not predictive of excess future returns. Going long high dividend yield stocks while going short low dividend yield stocks has not historically produced alpha.

Conversely, dividend stocks can indicate a stock with a low valuation or high quality, given dividend payers typically generate positive cash flow. Dividend yield investing is really just a watered-down version of value and quality investing - and a poor one at that.

Empirical data shows that an investor is likely to earn higher returns by focusing on a stock's valuation and/or quality, based on measures such as free cash flow and return on capital, instead of dividend yield.

Let's look at the numbers:

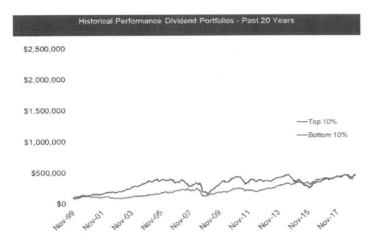

Source: Accelerate, S&P Capital IQ, Compustat

Over the past 20 years, Canadian stocks in the bottom 10% of dividend yield would have performed essentially the same as the top 10% of dividend yielders at 8% per annum. A $100,000 investment into either the highest dividend yielders or the lowest would have been worth $450,000 after 20 years.

While both top and bottom decile dividend yielders outperformed the TSX Composite by about 1% per year over that time frame, both sets of dividend yielders got crushed by low valuation and high-quality stocks.

109

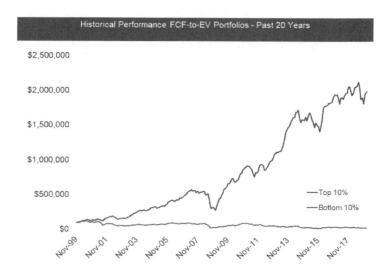

Source: Accelerate, S&P Capital IQ, Compustat

The top decile of FCF-to-EV stock portfolio, made up of stocks with low valuations based on free cash flow, would have compounded at 16% annualized, double the dividend portfolio. A $100,000 portfolio would have exceeded $2 million after 20 years. The bottom decile FCF-to-EV portfolio would have lost nearly -5% annually and a $100,000 portfolio based on the highest valuation stocks ended up at only $38,000.

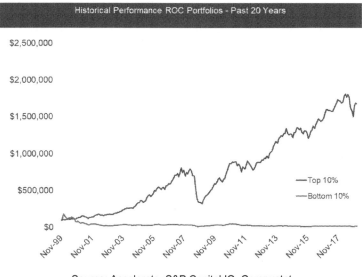

Source: Accelerate, S&P Capital IQ, Compustat

The top decile quality portfolio, made up of stocks exhibiting high return on capital, compounded at 15% per annum over the past 20 years. A $100,000 investment in the top 10% quality portfolio would grow to nearly $1.7 million after 20 years. The bottom 10% quality portfolio, made up of stocks with the worst return on capital, fell over -8% annually over 20 years and lost over 80% of the investor's portfolio over 20 years.

In contrast to the dividend portfolios, the divergence between the top decile value and quality portfolios compared to the bottom decile really points to the robustness and effectiveness of the factors. Empirical evidence indicates that focusing on valuation and quality of

111

securities will deliver higher total returns compared to investing based on dividends alone.

But What About My Much-Needed Income?

Investors can be hurt when blindly chasing dividend yields. Instead of focusing on dividend yield, investors should focus on total return. Valuation and quality-based measures offer a better model to generate total return compared to investing based on dividend yields, as seen above.

Total return is inclusive of both capital appreciation and dividends. The "income" an investor receives should be viewed through the lens of total return. An investor can generate income by harvesting capital gains. One should be indifferent to $1 from dividends or $1 from capital appreciation. Instead of utilizing only dividend payments, investors can pay themselves out of total return. The best part of this strategy is that it's more tax efficient, as capital gains are typically taxed at a lower rate than dividends.

Dividend Yield? Forget About It

Dividends have lost their luster ever since share buybacks came to dominate shareholder yield over the past 15 years. Combine this with the viewpoint that dividend yield investing is just a watered-down version of value and quality investing, albeit a much worse version.

If you insist on sticking with a yield-based investment strategy, invest based on free cash flow yield and quality instead of dividend yield. Your net worth will thank you later.

13

The Shareholder Yield Dilemma: Dividends or Share Buybacks?

Share buybacks have a much better track record of predictive outperformance than dividends.

We had previously warned investors not to invest in stocks based on their dividend yields in "Whatever You Do, Don't Invest Based On Dividend Yield." [31] In the piece, we posited that "dividends have lost their luster ever since share buybacks came to dominate shareholder yield over the past 15 years".

The S&P 500's share buyback yield is nearly 4%, almost double the index's dividend yield of 2%. Given that buybacks now account for two-thirds of the S&P 500's shareholder yield of 6%, the buyback yield is a far larger determinant in the success of an investment as compared to dividend yield. The terms buybacks and repurchases are used interchangeably.

Buyback Yield Yes, Dividend Yield No

Turns out, not only are share repurchases a much larger and more important portion of shareholder yield, share buybacks are a much better predictive factor of future equity performance as compared to dividends.

---

[31] Klymochko, Julian. "Whatever You Do, Don't Invest Based on Dividend Yield," Accelerate, 2019, https://accelerateshares.com/blog/whatever-you-do-dont-invest-based-on-dividend-yield/

Let's look at the numbers produced from a historical simulation of monthly-rebalanced buyback yield portfolios in both Canada and the U.S.

A portfolio of top decile share re-purchasers in Canada, meaning the top 10% of companies that most aggressively bought back their own shares, returned nearly 1,400% over the past 20 years. This represents a compound annual growth rate of 14.4% per annum.

A portfolio of the bottom 10% ranked stocks by share buybacks, or those companies *issuing* the most shares (the opposite of buying them back), returned only 50% over the past 20 years, representing a compound annual growth rate of just over 2% per year.

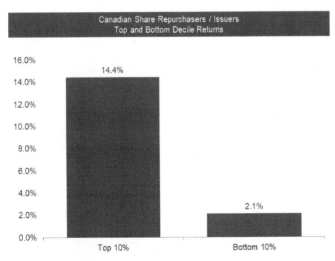

Source: Accelerate, S&P Capital IQ, Compustat

A $100,000 investment into a portfolio of the top 10% of share repurchasers in Canada would have grown to $1.5 million over 20 years.

Meanwhile, the same $100,000 investment into a portfolio of the bottom 10% of share re-purchasers (meaning the largest *issuers* of stock, or those with a negative buyback yield) would have grown to just $150,000 over the 20-year time frame.

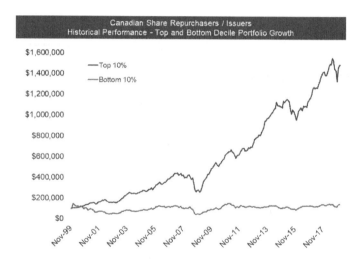

Source: Accelerate, S&P Capital IQ, Compustat

We see a similar dynamic in the performance of U.S. share re-purchasers and equity issuers.

A portfolio of the top 10% of U.S. stocks buying back their shares has seen a 946% return over the past 20 years, representing a 12.5% annualized return. A $100,000 investment into this portfolio would have grown to over $1 million over 20 years.

A portfolio of the bottom 10% of U.S. stocks ranked by share repurchases, or those with the greatest negative buyback yield (net share issuers) would have seen a -23% loss over the past 20 years (-1.2% annualized), turning a $100,000 investment into just $77,000.

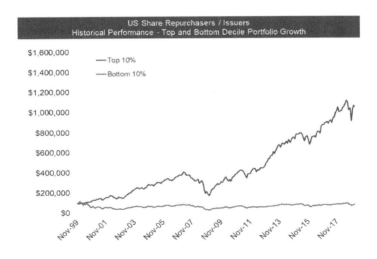

Source: Accelerate, S&P Capital IQ, Compustat

Clearly, there's a large divergence between the top and bottom decile ranked share buyback portfolios in both geographical markets. This means that the share buyback

119

factor could be deemed robust and could perhaps be expected to have reasonable predictive ability.

Contrast this to the performance of dividend-ranked portfolios. Looking at a portfolio of the top 10% Canadian dividend payers, or those stocks that pay the highest dividend yield, it performed in line with a portfolio of the bottom 10% of dividend payers at approximately 8% per year, over the past 20 years.

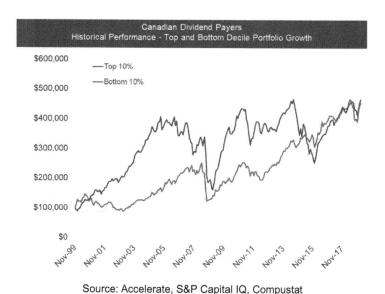

Source: Accelerate, S&P Capital IQ, Compustat

A similar historical performance was notched by top and bottom U.S. dividend yield portfolios over the past 20 years. The top decile, highest yielding dividend portfolio returned

8.2% per annum while the bottom decile, or lowest yielding dividend portfolio returned 7.0% per annum.

Source: Accelerate, S&P Capital IQ, Compustat

Not only did the top dividend yield portfolios underperform the top share buyback portfolios by 6.4% and 4.3% per year in Canada and the U.S., respectively, over the past 20 years, there was really no material divergence in performance between the top and bottom decile dividend yield portfolios.

This means that dividend yield is really not a robust factor because one cannot create a market-neutral portfolio, being

121

long top decile dividend yielders and short bottom decile yielders, which produces material alpha.

Buybacks for The Win

There are two salient points to note in the buybacks versus dividends debate in investing:

1. As a proportion of shareholder yield, buybacks are a far larger share of capital being returned to shareholders, and therefore buyback yield should be a much more important factor to consider when analyzing a stock and the company's capital allocation with respect to shareholder yield.

2. The top decile portfolio of share re-purchasers has outperformed the top decile portfolio of dividend payers, while also displaying a substantially larger divergence in performance between the factor's top and bottom decile portfolios. Said simply, buybacks have a much better track record of predictive outperformance than dividends.

Bottom line? When considering the shareholder yield conundrum, focus on a stock's share buyback yield and ignore its dividend yield.

14

Stocks With a "Hot Hand"— Investing with Operating Momentum

When a public company has a hot hand and its performance continues to exceed expectations, its stock should be bought.

The "hot hand" phenomenon occurs when a person who experiences a successful attempt has a greater chance, or positive momentum, in successful further attempts.

There were plenty of hot hands in the Toronto Raptors' clinching of the 2019 NBA Championship. A prime example of the hot hand phenomenon was Raptors' star forward Kawhi Leonard's performance throughout the playoffs. Whether it be his series-clinching, 3-point buzzer beater against the Philadelphia 76ers, or his 10-0 run in game 5 of the finals against the venerable Golden State Warriors, Kawhi's positive momentum showed that basketball is one of the most common areas in which the hot hand phenomenon is displayed.

When a shooter has the hot hand, give him the ball. When a gambler keeps hitting winning bets, double down.

There's an investing analogy too. When a public company keeps beating capital markets' expectations, buy the stock!

A Stock's Hot Hand - Operating Momentum

A stock can have a hot hand, or positive operating momentum, when the company's fundamental operating performance continues to exceed the expectations of the market.

There are a number of ways to measure a public company's operating momentum. Two of our preferred operating momentum metrics include:

1. Consensus EPS Revisions: The change in consensus earnings per share (EPS) expectations over time.

2. Earnings Abnormal Returns: Abnormal share price performance after the release of quarterly results.

A 20-year performance simulation was run to test these operating momentum factors. The simulations ran two model factor portfolios: one that invested in the top 10% (i.e., highest operating momentum) and one that invested in the bottom 10% (i.e., lowest operating momentum) portfolios of stocks ranked by operating momentum, rebalanced on a monthly basis in both Canada and the U.S.

This empirical data indicates that stocks with positive operating momentum, as measured through high Consensus EPS Revisions or positive Earnings Abnormal Returns, outperform stocks with negative operating momentum.

When EPS Estimates Keep Heading Higher

You know things are going well for a company when analysts are constantly raising their earnings estimates. Conversely, when analysts are lowering their earnings forecasts for a company, then things are likely going poorly. The share price tends to follow.

The Consensus EPS Revisions factor ranks stocks based on the month-over-month change in average analyst earnings per share estimate. The data show that the top decile of stocks whose underlying earnings estimates are increasing vastly outperform the bottom decile of stocks, or those whose earnings estimates are decreasing the most.

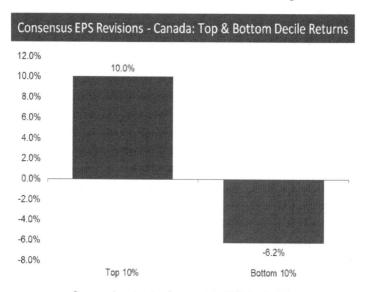

Source: Accelerate, Compustat, S&P Capital IQ

126

Over the past 20 years, the portfolio of the top 10% highest operating momentum stocks in Canada as measured by rising EPS revisions, rebalanced on a monthly basis, returned 10.0% annually. Over the same time period, the portfolio of the bottom 10% of stocks having the most negative EPS revisions lost -6.2% per year.

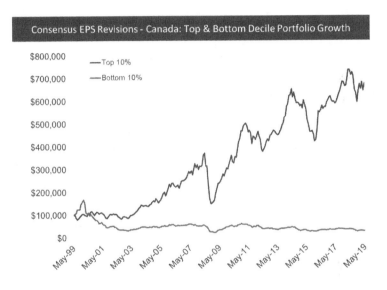

Source: Accelerate, Compustat, S&P Capital IQ

If one were to invest $100,000 in the top decile operating momentum portfolio in Canada, after 20 years it would have grown to almost $700,000. That same $100,000 invested in the bottom decile operating momentum portfolio would have shrunk to under $30,000, a loss of nearly -75%.

127

The Consensus EPS Revisions factor performance was not as significant in the U.S. as in Canada, but the long portfolio of top decile operating momentum stocks still has positive performance and vastly outperformed the negative-returning bottom decile portfolio, as seen below.

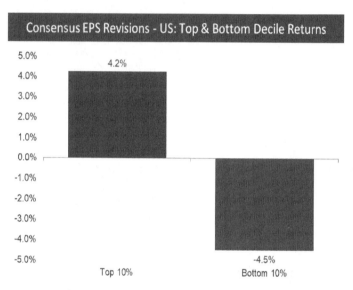

Source: Accelerate, Compustat, S&P Capital IQ

Over the past two decades, the portfolio holding the top 10% of U.S. stocks with the highest upward EPS revisions returned 4.2% per year, while the bottom 10% of stocks, those with the most negative EPS revisions, declined by -4.5% per year.

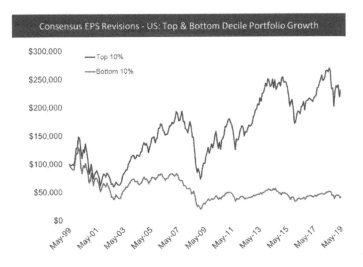

Source: Accelerate, Compustat, S&P Capital IQ

A $100,000 investment in the top 10% of U.S. stocks as measured by increasing EPS revisions would have more than doubled over 20 years while a $100,000 investment in the bottom 10% of U.S. stocks with the most negative EPS revisions would have declined to less than $40,000.

When A Stock Rallies Post Earnings

The "beat and raise" finance parlance for when a company exceeds analyst expectations of quarterly performance and also raises guidance for near-term future performance, is typically accompanied by a stock price rally.

Earnings Abnormal Returns refers to the abnormal positive (negative) share price performance that occurs when a company's quarterly financial performance exceeds (falls short of) expectations.

The data show that companies whose shares rally after reporting their quarterly financial results (i.e., positive abnormal share price returns) typically keep going up while companies whose shares fall after releasing their quarterly reports tend to keep falling. Companies that "beat and raise" tend to continue to do so.

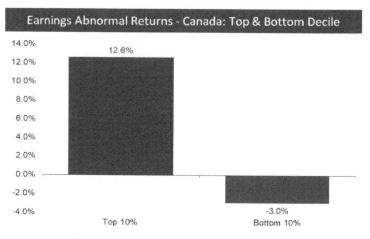

Source: Accelerate, Compustat, S&P Capital IQ

Over the 20-year simulation, the portfolio of Canadian stocks ranking in the top decile of Earnings Abnormal Returns compounded at 12.6% per year while the portfolio of bottom decile stocks with the most negative abnormal returns around their quarterly results lost -3.0% per year.

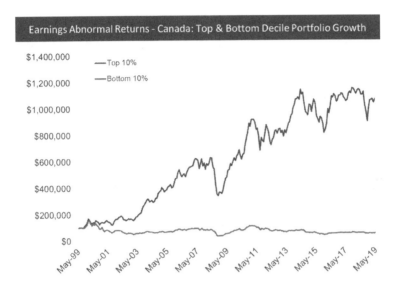

Source: Accelerate, Compustat, S&P Capital IQ

A $100,000 investment in the portfolio of top decile stocks ranked by Earnings Abnormal Returns would have grown to approximately $1,000,000 over 20 years. Comparatively, a $100,000 investment into the bottom 10% of stocks ranked by Earnings Abnormal Returns would have declined to less than $60,000.

The performance of the operating momentum factor as measured by Earnings Abnormal Returns in the U.S. was not as pronounced as in Canada, however, the U.S.

portfolios did exhibit substantial alpha, or performance spread, between the top 10% and bottom the 10% ranked stocks.

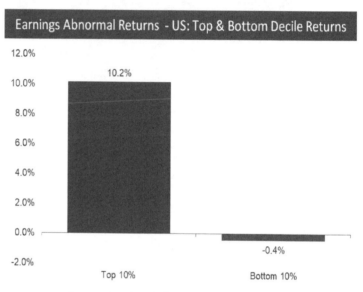

Source: Accelerate, Compustat, S&P Capital IQ

The top decile ranking of U.S. stocks with good operating momentum gained 10.2% annualized over the past 20 years. Comparatively, the bottom decile of U.S stocks, or those with the worst operating momentum as measured by Earnings Abnormal Returns, lost -0.4% per year.

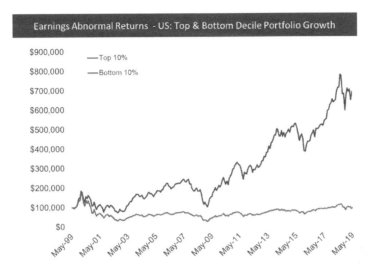

Source: Accelerate, Compustat, S&P Capital IQ

An investment of $100,000 in that top decile of U.S. stock based on Earnings Abnormal Returns operating momentum would have grown to nearly $700,000 compared to the same investment in the bottom decile of U.S. stocks, which would have shrunk to about $92,000.

Operating Momentum – Alpha On The Short Side

Over the same time period of the simulations, the past 20 years, the S&P / TSX Composite had an annualized total return of 6.9% while the S&P 500 total return was 5.8%.

All of the long top decile portfolios based on operating momentum beat the market, except Consensus EPS Revisions in the U.S.

However, the most interesting aspect of the data is not how much the top 10% ranked stock portfolios beat the market on average, but how much the bottom 10% ranked stock portfolios underperformed. This indicates that an enterprising investor could generate substantial alpha, or outperformance, by short selling these bottom ranked operating momentum stocks. This is a key insight that smart beta (long-only) investors miss.

Is The Hot Hand Phenomenon A Fallacy? I Think Not

While long believed to be a fallacy, the hot hand in basketball is now thought of to exist given more recent advanced statistical studies based on additional empirical evidence.

Just as the data supports the hot hand phenomenon in basketball, empirical evidence shows that the hot hand phenomenon exists in stocks, as manifested through a company's operating momentum. Some key operating momentum characteristics include Consensus EPS Revisions and Earnings Abnormal Returns.

When a public company has a hot hand and its performance continues to exceed expectations, its stock should be bought. Conversely, when a stock is cold with poor operating momentum, it should be sold or even shorted.

Invest with a hot hand and take operating momentum into account.

15

Does Investing in High-Quality Stocks Work? Why Yes. Yes, It Does.

---

*Own only high-quality stocks
and short only low-quality stocks.*

"Own only high-quality stocks" is an oft-repeated investment mantra.

We can take this investment maxim one step further and say the goal for an investor is to not only own stocks that are high quality but to not own, or even short sell, stocks that are low quality.

But what exactly is a high- or low-quality stock?

The Blue Chips

According to Wall Street folklore, one day during the 1920's Dow Jones employee Oliver Gingold was watching the ticker tape. Oliver noticed a number of stocks trading at prices above $200 per share and took note. He made the analogy that in poker, the blue chips have the highest value out of all the poker chips, and christened these high-priced stocks equivalent to the high-priced blue chips in poker.

Feeling that these high-priced stocks may be exceptional, Oliver told Lucien Hooper of brokerage firm W.E. Hutton & Co. that he planned to return to his office to start writing (now known as blogging) about "these blue-chip stocks".

Originally used to refer to high-priced stocks just as blue chips in poker carry higher values, the parlance has evolved such that blue chips now indicate stocks of high quality.

How To Measure Quality

There are numerous metrics used to measure the quality of an investment including profit margins, growth rates, balance sheet health, return on equity, accruals, etc. In fact, there is a litany of quantitative factors that could potentially measure the quality of a stock.

After analyzing and testing the vast majority of these quality factors from both a quantitative and qualitative perspective, we determined that two of the best metrics to measure the quality of a stock are:

- Return on Capital (ROC) defined as Operating Income / Invested Capital; and,
- Gross Profits / Assets (GP/A).

A 20-year simulation was run to test these quality factors. The simulations ran two model factor portfolios: one that invested in the top 10% (i.e., high quality) and one that invested in the bottom 10% (i.e., low quality) portfolios of quality stocks, rebalanced on a monthly basis in both Canada and the U.S. The end result?

The portfolios of high-quality stocks generated tremendous returns while the portfolios of low-quality stocks generated large losses.

ROC-ing Out

Return on Capital (ROC) measures how efficiently a company can generate operating profits given its capitalization. A company with a high ROC is generating substantial operating profit off of its capital (typically equity and debt capital) and would be considered high quality, while a company with low ROC is typically generating losses and would be considered low quality. You would rather invest in the former rather than the latter, right? Let's look at the numbers on the tail ends of the distribution, specifically the top and bottom 10%.

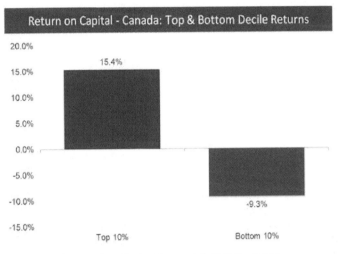

Source: Accelerate, Compustat, S&P Capital IQ

Over the past 20 years, the portfolio of the top 10% highest quality Canadian stocks as measured by ROC, rebalanced on a monthly basis, returned 15.4% annually. A $100,000 investment in the top decile of quality stocks would have turned into $1.7 million. Over the same time frame, the portfolio of the bottom 10% of stocks having the lowest ROC lost -9.3% per year. That same $100,000 investment in the lowest ROC, or the bottom decile quality, stocks would have shrunk to about $15,000.

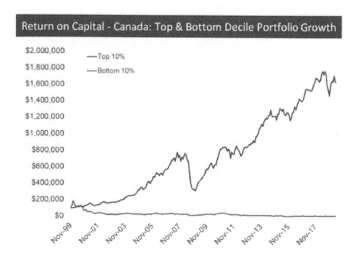

Source: Accelerate, Compustat, S&P Capital IQ

We see a similar dynamic in the U.S. where high quality, top decile ROC stock portfolios dramatically outperformed the bottom decile, lowest ROC, quality portfolios.

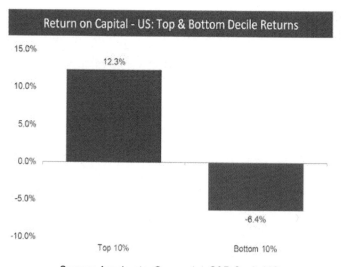

Source: Accelerate, Compustat, S&P Capital IQ

142

Over the past 20 years, the top decile quality U.S stock portfolio returned 12.3% annually, while the bottom decile ROC or lowest quality portfolio lost -6.4% annually.

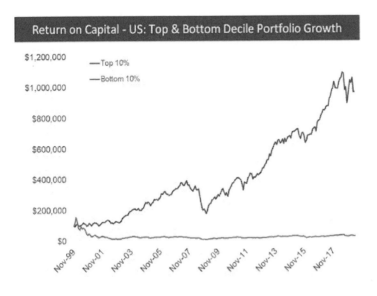

Source: Accelerate, Compustat, S&P Capital IQ

A $100,000 investment in the top 10% high ROC U.S. stock portfolio would have grown to over $1 million while a $100,000 investment in the bottom 10% low ROC U.S. stock portfolio would have shriveled to just under $27,000.

"Enough to make you throw up, man, it's gross what I net" – Drake

Gross profits are anything but. In fact, they're quite sweet – gross profits are the difference between a company's revenue and its cost of goods sold. The bigger, the better. When looked at as a percentage of a company's assets, Gross Profits / Assets or GP/A, measures how well a company can sell goods or services profitably from its asset base. As a measure of a business' efficiency, GP/A is closely related to ROC.

Unsurprisingly, stocks possessing a high GP/A, a characteristic of high-quality stocks, have generated significant share price outperformance. Conversely, stocks with a low GP/A have underperformed dramatically.

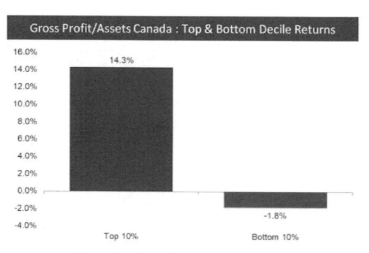

Source: Accelerate, Compustat, S&P Capital IQ

In Canada, a portfolio of the top decile quality stocks as measured by GP/A compounded at 14.3% per year over the past 20 years. A portfolio of the bottom decile quality stocks, or those with the lowest GP/A, lost -1.8% per year.

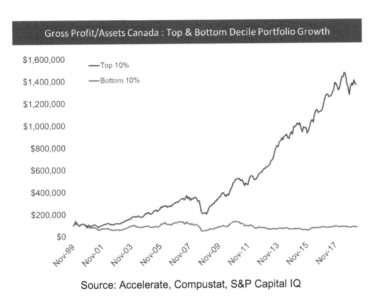

Source: Accelerate, Compustat, S&P Capital IQ

A $100,000 investment in a portfolio of top decile GP/A quality stocks in Canada would have turned into over $1.4 million over the past 20 years while the same $100,000 invested in a portfolio of bottom decile GP/A Canadian stocks would have declined to about $70,000.

As one would expect, we see a similar result in U.S. equities. A portfolio of high-quality GP/A U.S. stocks generated substantial outperformance while a portfolio of low-quality GP/A equities underperformed markedly.

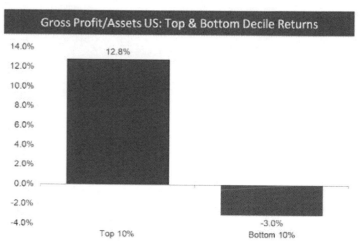

Source: Accelerate, Compustat, S&P Capital IQ

In the U.S., a portfolio of top decile GP/A stocks returned 12.8% over the past two decades while the bottom decile portfolio, or lowest quality stocks, lost -3.0% per year.

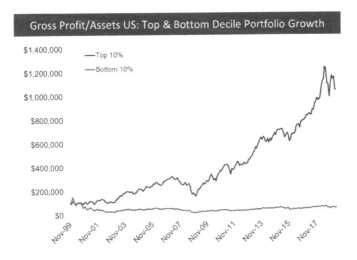

Source: Accelerate, Compustat, S&P Capital IQ

Similar to the other top decile quality portfolio performances, a $100,000 investment in a portfolio of the top U.S. quality stocks as determined by GP/A grew to over $1 million over the past 20 years. The bottom decile portfolio of low-quality U.S. stocks struggled, with a $100,000 investment losing nearly half its value over the two decades.

Top Quality All Day

As the data shows, the investment maxim "own only high-quality stocks" has been proven correct. However, given the substantial underperformance of low-quality stocks, we may need to add to the quality investing mantra:

"Own only high-quality stocks and short only low-quality stocks".

16

The Trend is Your Friend: Long-Short Investing Using the Trend Factor

---

The trend is your friend when it comes to stocks - consider being long stocks with a positive trend and if you're up for it, short stocks with a negative trend.

From skinny jeans to aviator sunglasses, modern fashion is littered with trends - some a flash-in-the-pan and some enduring.

From fashion to economics, trends are often analyzed and extrapolated to make forecasts and predictions. While retailers are always trying to figure out what will be the hot new fashion trend, stock analysts are always analyzing stock trends to try to forecast returns.

One powerful methodology of measuring the trend in a stock is to look at the relative daily moving averages of the price. Specifically, looking at how a stock's 50-day moving average compares to its 200-day moving average. A stock's 50-day moving average refers to the average closing price over the past 50 days while the 200-day moving average refers to the stock's average closing price over the past 200 trading sessions.

When a stock's 50-day moving average is above its 200-day moving average, it has a positive trend. Conversely, a stock has a negative trend if its 50-day moving average is below its 200-day moving average. There's a reason that technical analysts call it a "golden cross" when a stock's 50-day moving average moves above its 200-day moving average and a "death cross" when the 50-day moves below the 200-

day. While the nomenclature isn't important, the trend certainly is.

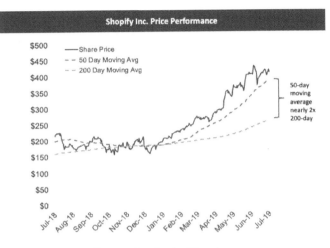

Source: Accelerate, Bloomberg

The share price graph above plots Shopify's 1-year return, along with its 50-day and 200-day moving averages. In this example, the 50-day is nearly 2x the 200-day moving average, which denotes a bullish trend. Due to in part its positive trend, we would be long (buying) the stock.

Historically, stocks with the best trend, or the stocks whose 50-day moving average is furthest above their 200-day moving average, have had the highest returns. In addition, stocks with the worst trend, or those whose 50-day moving average is furthest below their 200-day moving average, have suffered the biggest losses.

This was tested through a 20-year simulation on both Canadian and U.S. stocks. Each month, all stocks were ranked and sorted into deciles based on the ratio of their 50-day moving average compared to their 200-day moving average. The top 10% of stocks with the best trend were grouped into decile 1, while the next best 10% of stocks based on their trends were grouped into decile 2, and so on.

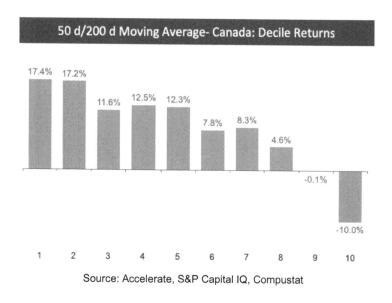

Source: Accelerate, S&P Capital IQ, Compustat

The simulated 20-year annualized returns for each decile are plotted above. The portfolio of stocks with the best trend, decile 1, returned 17.4% annually over the past 20 years. The next best 10% portfolio of stocks, decile 2, returned 17.2% per year. Generally, the higher the trend ranking, the higher the return. For example, decile 1 (the top decile) outperforms all other trend deciles.

The trend factor is most noticeable at the tails – specifically the top and bottom 10% trend portfolios. The true power of the trend factor is accentuated when we focus on the extremes.

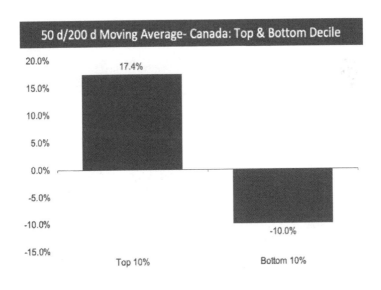

Source: Accelerate, S&P Capital IQ, Compustat

In Canada, the top decile trend portfolio returned 17.4% annualized over the past 20 years, while the bottom decile trend portfolio lost -10.0% annually. The spread between the top and bottom trend decile clocked in at 27.4% per year, a very high spread differential between the performance of the top and bottom decile trend portfolios.

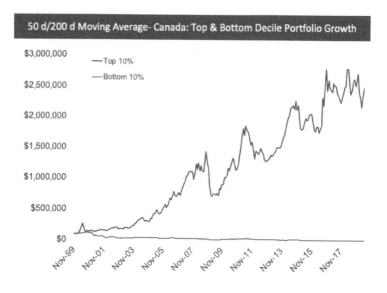

50 d/200 d Moving Average- Canada: Top & Bottom Decile Portfolio Growth

Source: Accelerate, S&P Capital IQ, Compustat

A $100,000 investment in the top decile trend portfolio in Canada 20 years ago would have grown into nearly $2.5 million. This same $100,000 invested in the bottom decile Canadian trend portfolio would have shrunk to about $12,000, a loss of nearly -90%. Clearly, paying attention to trending stocks is useful in both long and short (selling) investing.

The simulated trend portfolios show a similar result in the U.S. as well, with top trend portfolios dramatically outperforming while the lousy bottom trend portfolios lose money.

Source: Accelerate, S&P Capital IQ, Compustat

U.S. stocks exhibit a similar profile to their Canadian brethren – portfolios of stocks with the best trend have the highest returns, while the portfolios of stocks with the worst trends suffered the worst performance.

Again, we see the most extreme outperformance and underperformance in the tails. The top decile portfolio of stocks with the best trend outperformed while the bottom decile of stocks with the worst trend underperformed significantly.

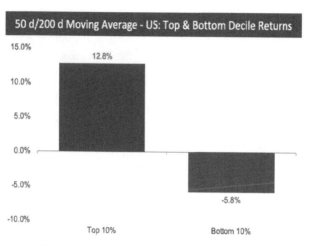

Source: Accelerate, S&P Capital IQ, Compustat

Over the past two decades, the portfolio of top ranked trend stocks (top 10%) in the U.S. compounded at 12.8% annually. Over the same time frame, the portfolio of the bottom ranked trend stocks (bottom 10%) in the U.S. lost -5.8% per year. The spread differential between the two portfolios was 18.6% per year.

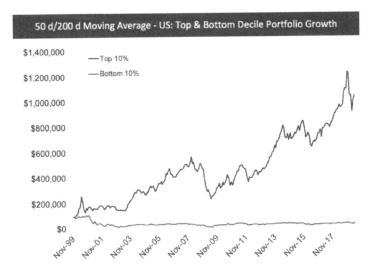

Source: Accelerate, S&P Capital IQ, Compustat

A $100,000 investment into the top decile trend portfolio in the U.S. would have grown to over $1 million over the past 20 years while the same amount invested into the bottom decile trend portfolio would have declined to less than $35,000 or lost over -65%.

What's an investor to do with this data? Clearly, one should focus on owning stocks with a positive trend. In addition, an investor should avoid owning stocks with a negative trend. Enterprising investors may even consider short-selling stocks exhibiting negative trends, in order to both hedge their long portfolios and generate additional performance from short selling.

We analyze and act based on trends in all areas of life. We shop for the hottest new trends to stock our closets and eat food based on the hottest new diet to stay in shape. Don't exclude trends from your investing. The trend is your friend when it comes to stocks - consider being long stocks with a positive trend and if you're up for it, short stocks with a negative trend.

17

What Happens When We Combine Value and Momentum?

An investor can combine the value and momentum factors to create a powerful, Voltron-like multi-factor that can lead to the supercharging of investment returns.

One hundred and ten years ago, a successful laboratory experiment run by chemist Fritz Haber revolutionized the agricultural industry worldwide. In the experiment, Haber placed osmium in a steel chamber, pumped in a combination of both hydrogen and nitrogen gas, then applied pressure and heat. The result of the experiment was an outflow of ammonia, the raw material used to produce synthetic fertilizer.

Scientists had known that nitrogen was crucial for plant life, but prior to Haber's experiment, there was no known way to produce it. The process of synthesizing and manufacturing ammonia from combining hydrogen and nitrogen, known as the Haber-Bosch process, was one of the most important technological discoveries of the 20th century. This synthesis of ammonia enabled widespread use of fertilizer, which substantially improved crop yields globally and provided more food for a rapidly growing global population. As a result, the world's population rocketed from 1.6 billion to 6 billion over the 20th century.

This process of combining two unremarkable and ubiquitous elements into a new, far more practical compound is akin to modern-day alchemy.

The Haber-Bosch analogy can be applied to modern-day investing, by taking two common investment factors, value and momentum, and combining them to form a multi-factor model that results in higher risk-adjusted returns for an investor.

Value - Buy Dirt Cheap Stocks

The value factor was first noted by Ben Graham and David Dodd in their 1934 book *Security Analysis*. A core concept in the text was that of a margin of safety, which referred to buying a stock at a discount to its intrinsic value. The notion of a margin of safety is synonymous with value investing.

In practice, value investing refers to buying a security at a discounted price. This discounted price is typically discerned by looking at various valuation metrics such as book-to-market, earnings yield or EBITDA-to-EV (where EBITDA stands for Earnings before interest, tax, depreciation and amortization and EV refers to Enterprise value).

We previously detailed why cash-flow-based valuation measures such as EBITDA-to-EV are preferred to book equity measures such as book-to-market and earnings measures such as earnings yield in the chapter, *Value Investing Is Dead! #FAKENEWS.* [32]

The reason EBITDA-to-EV is preferred for a value factor? Performance, of course.

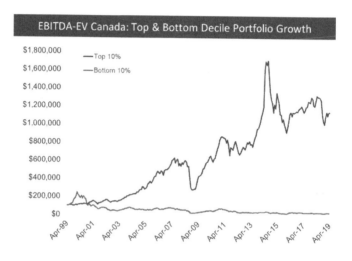

Source: Accelerate, S&P Capital IQ, Compustat

Over the past 20 years, a portfolio of the top 10% of Canadian stocks based on EBITDA-to-EV, meaning the cheapest stocks, returned 12.9% annually. Over the same time frame, a portfolio of the bottom decile stocks value stocks, or those with the highest valuations based on

---

[32] Klymochko, Julian. "Value Investing Is Dead! #FAKENEWS," Accelerate, 2019, https://accelerateshares.com/blog/value-investing-is-dead-fakenews/

EBITDA, returned -5.2% per year. These portfolios are rebalanced on a monthly basis.

The top decile Canadian value stocks returned 12.9% annually with volatility of 21.5%. This resulted in a Sharpe ratio, or return per unit of risk, of 0.6.

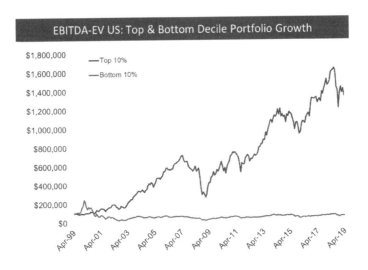

Source: Accelerate, S&P Capital IQ, Compustat

In the U.S. market over the past 20 years, the top decile of value stocks (i.e., the cheapest) based on EBITDA-to-EV returned 13.9% annually, while the bottom decile (i.e., most expensive) returned -2.0% per year.

The top decile U.S. value stocks returned 13.9% per year with volatility of 22.7%, resulting in a Sharpe ratio of 0.6.

163

Historical performance shows that EBITDA-to-EV is a more robust factor in predicting future equity returns. Investors who would have utilized this metric could have generated impressive returns.

It's no surprise that an entire industry, known as private equity, has grown from the use of the EBITDA multiple (the inverse of the EBITDA-to-EV metric). The private equity industry, borne of buying cheapest companies based on EBITDA and combining it with leverage, has now grown to a staggering $3.5 trillion in assets. The main driver in this breakneck growth has been performance, which can be mainly attributed to the EBITDA multiple in combination with leverage.

Momentum - Buy High Sell Higher

The momentum factor has been favoured by market traders and speculators for over a century. It was the preferred factor of famed speculator Jesse Livermore in the 1920's, as detailed in Edwin Lefevre's 1923 literary classic "Reminiscences of a Stock Operator". I shamelessly named this book "Reminiscences of a Hedge Fund Operator" as a tribute to this classic.

One of Livermore's rules of trading was to buy rising stocks and sell falling stocks.

This 52-week high momentum factor can be implemented by segmenting stocks based on how close to their 52-week high closing price they are trading. To hold a momentum portfolio, the stocks closest to their 52-week highs are to be bought.

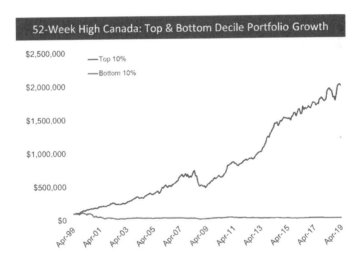

Source: Accelerate, S&P Capital IQ, Compustat

A portfolio of the top decile of Canadian stocks closest to their 52-week highs compounded at 16.1% annually over the past 20 years. The lowest 10% portfolio of stocks furthest from their 52-week highs lost -11.3% per year over the same time frame, costing investors nearly their entire investments.

The top decile of Canadian momentum stocks returned 16.1% annually over the past 20 years with volatility of only 12.0%, resulting in a Sharpe ratio of 1.3.

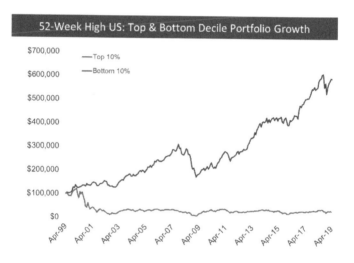

Source: Accelerate, S&P Capital IQ, Compustat

As for U.S. stocks, the top 10% of stocks with the best momentum based on their proximity to their 52-week highs, returned 9.3% annually over the past 20 years. A portfolio of the bottom 10% of momentum stocks, or those furthest from their 52-week highs, lost -5.5% per year.

The top decile of U.S. momentum stocks returned 9.3% annually over the past two decades with a volatility of 12.6%, resulting in a Sharpe ratio of 0.7.

Value And Momentum - They Form Like Voltron

In the 1980's there was an animated television series called Voltron. It featured a team of space explorers that each piloted a robot lion vehicle. Each of these explorers were powerful on their own, but when required they would combine their robots to form super-robot Voltron, a powerful force.

Value and momentum are powerful in their own right. When combined, these factors can form like Voltron into a powerful multi-factor.

The result of this Voltron-esque combination of value and momentum? Better risk-adjusted returns.

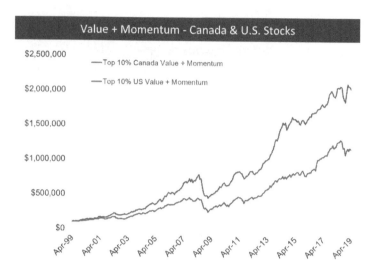

Source: Accelerate, S&P Capital IQ, Compustat

	Canadian Stocks		
	EBITDA-EV	52-Week High	Value + Momentum
Return	12.9%	16.1%	16.2%
Volatility	21.4%	12.0%	12.5%
Sharpe	0.6	1.3	1.3

	US Stocks		
	EBITDA-EV	52-Week High	Value + Momentum
Return	13.9%	9.3%	13.0%
Volatility	22.7%	12.6%	14.2%
Sharpe	0.6	0.7	0.9

Source: Accelerate, S&P Capital IQ, Compustat

When the value and momentum factors are combined in Canada, the result is the highest returning portfolio at 16.2% over the past 20 years. On a risk-adjusted basis, the combined portfolio's Sharpe, or return per unit of risk, ties the momentum strategy at 1.3.

In the U.S., when the value and momentum factors are combined, the result is the highest risk-adjusted return with a Sharpe of 0.9.

Valuementum

Chemist Fritz Haber combined nitrogen and hydrogen to form ammonia, which revolutionized agriculture and led to the supercharging of human population growth.

Similarly, an investor can combine the value and momentum factors to create a powerful, Voltron-like multi-factor that can lead to the supercharging of investment returns.

18

Innovators, Imitators, and Idiots

It's good to be influenced by great investors and study their methodologies and techniques, but ultimately, to find success in investing an investor must find his or her own style.

Warren Buffett and his business partner Charlie Munger became billionaires through stock market investing. The long-time business partners who head up the investment conglomerate Berkshire Hathaway have generated market-beating returns for many decades utilizing their value + quality mantra to invest in companies with sustainable competitive advantages (i.e., "moats") at attractive prices.

Unsurprisingly, their investment success has been heavily replicated over the years. In 1986, 1,000 people attended Berkshire Hathaway's annual meeting (the so-called "Woodstock for Capitalists"). In 2017, over 42,000 people attended the event[33]. Warren Buffett's annual letter to shareholders, released each February, is read by thousands or even millions of investors. Every move Berkshire makes is dissected by countless analysts and market pundits. Google "Warren Buffett" and you'll get 28.6 million results. A search for "Berkshire Hathaway" nets 45.4 million. Warren and Charlie's investment process has been meticulously analyzed and detailed in a myriad of books, studies, blog posts and articles.

---

[33] Imbert, Fred. "Berkshire shareholders go to Omaha to get as much Buffett and Munger as they can," CNBC, 2018, https://www.cnbc.com/2018/05/05/shareholders-try-to-get-as-much-buffett-and-munger-as-they-can.html

Basically, Warren Buffett is the Bret Hart of investing[34] - "The Best There Is, the Best There Was, the Best There Ever Will Be".

According to Berkshire's 2017 annual report[35], its stock has compounded at 20.9% annually since 1965 for a total gain of 2,404,748%. Over that time frame, the S&P 500 has compounded at 9.9% for a total gain of 15,508%. Clearly, their investment technique works and it works exceptionally well!

Since inception, Berkshire has handily outperformed the S&P 500 over any 10-year time frame. That is until recently.

For the 10 years ending February 2019, Berkshire had a 292.5% total return. It was beaten by the S&P 500 ETF, which returned 330.6% over the past 10 years.

[34] "Bret "Hit Man" Hart: The Best There Is, the Best There Was, the Best There Ever Will Be," Wikipedia, 2019, https://en.wikipedia.org/wiki/Bret_%22Hit_Man%22_Hart:_The_Best_There_Is,_the_Best_There_Was,_the_Best_There_Ever_Will_Be
[35] "Berkshire Hathaway Inc. 2017 Annual Report," 2017, http://www.berkshirehathaway.com/2017ar/2017ar.pdf

Source: Bloomberg

Berkshire failed to even beat the broad stock market index over the past decade, which it used to do with ease.

What happened?

Did Warren and Charlie lose their touch?

Did Berkshire grow too big?

Did their investment methods stop outperforming?

When an investment methodology, such as Berkshire's value + quality strategy, gets replicated by too many copycats, it tends to stop working. While the size of Berkshire certainly is a limiting factor in its outperformance, no doubt when too many other investors began mimicking

174

Berkshire's investment process, its outperformance began to decline.

The always delightful Charlie Munger addressed this notion in the Wall Street Journal [36]:

> 'The money managers among them are "like a bunch of cod fishermen after all the cod's been overfished... They don't catch a lot of cod, but they keep on fishing in the same waters. That's what's happened to all these value investors. Maybe they should move to where the fish are."'
> -Berkshire Hathaway Vice Chairman Charlie Munger

There are hundreds of thousands of Buffett-wannabees. So many such that Berkshire's investment strategy has become heavily overfished by keen copycat analysts hoping to create the second coming of Berkshire.

So, what's an investor to do? Clearly, copying a heavily replicated strategy is not the answer. It's good to be influenced by great investors and study their methodologies

---

[36] Zweig, Jason. "When Charlie Munger Calls, Listen and Learn," The Wall Street Journal, 2019, https://www.wsj.com/articles/when-charlie-munger-calls-listen-and-learn-11548421209

and techniques, but ultimately, to find success, an investor must find his or her own style.

Buffett's "three I's" expresses this idea succinctly: First come the *innovators*, who create something unique and novel. Then come the *imitators*, who seek to copy the innovators. Finally come the *idiots*, whose greed tends to ruin what the innovators created.

Whether it be investing, business or any other pursuit, to truly find astounding success, one must be unique in their approach.

Be an innovator.

19

So, What Are You Waiting For?

No amount of study, analysis or even paper-trading can make up for real-world investing experience. Nothing focuses the mind and sears a lesson into your brain than losing money on an investment.

I loved playing video games as a kid. Back then, in the early 1990s, we still had arcades.

On a week-long family summer road trip in 1994, I spent most of my downtime while driving across the country in the back of our Volvo station wagon reading video game magazines.

One brand new arcade game that I was particularly excited about was called Killer Instinct. As you can tell by the name, it was about as violent as you'd expect - especially for an 11-year-old!

Nonetheless, I was keen on becoming good at the one-on-one combat arcade game. I used our 12-hour travel days sitting in the back of the car to meticulously study the attack combinations for my favourite characters. I felt that if I had all the combinations memorized, I would be unbeatable.

I must have spent dozens of hours memorizing the gameplay. As expected, I was so excited to finally get my chance to show off my Killer Instinct skills and knowledge at the local arcade when I got back home.

Stepping into the arcade with a pocket full of quarters, I spotted the game I had been itching to play over the last week. It was open too. I selected my favourite character and repeated his best combinations in my head before the match started.

It was go time! At last, time to show off the skills that I thought I had.

The problem was, I sucked! I couldn't execute any of the combinations; the movements felt foreign. I was getting destroyed, and all the knowledge I had felt completely useless.

I lost my first game badly. Man, was I discouraged. However, I learned an incredibly useful lesson: No amount of academic study can replicate the skills gained with real-world experience.

Nowhere is this lesson more applicable than in investing. No amount of study, analysis or even paper-trading can make up for real-world investing experience. Nothing focuses the mind and sears a lesson into your brain than losing money on an investment.

Hopefully my experiences and knowledge has helped open your mind to new mental models, investment strategies and variant views on the market.

One investing concept with a negative connotation that I particularly dislike is the concept of "style drift". Style drift refers to when investment managers participate in investment strategies outside of their initial wheelhouse.

What others refer to as style drift, I call progression. As a matter of fact, if you're not constantly improving your investment process and evolving as an investor, you are dead.

Essentially, all of today's great investors have evolved significantly from their original investment strategies in which they cut their teeth. Warren Buffett started out "cigar butt" investing and engaging in arbitrage and activism. Now he's a mainly a GARP (growth at a reasonable price) investor. Ken Griffin launched Citadel to trade a convertible arbitrage strategy and now it's one of the largest multi-strategy firms in the world. John Paulson was a merger arbitrageur who hit it big way outside of his wheelhouse - trading credit default swaps on synthetic CDOs (containing subprime mortgages) where he made billions of dollars. Jim Simons first started out fundamental investing before moving to model driven trading, and now his ultra-successful Renaissance Technologies hedge fund trades solely off some of the best quantitative investment strategies in the world.

I approach investing the same way athletes approach sports. You're not going to be the best basketball player if you can only slam dunk. In order to be the MVP, you need to excel at every aspect of the game. You need to be able to shoot jumpers, three pointers, dunk, dribble, pass, block and steal. A skilled practitioner uses all the tools he has in his toolkit.

Whether it is multi-factor investing, short-selling or arbitrage, hopefully my reminiscences as a hedge fund manager got you interested in additional techniques to further your investment skillset.

So, what are you waiting for?

References

[1] Sec. *Frequently Asked Questions & Answers,"* Bloomberg LP, 2018, https://www.sec.gov/Archives/edgar/data/1593034/00011931251537100 5/d81465dex992.htm

[2] Barr, Alistair & Newcomer, Eric. "SoftBank CEO Adds Driverless Tech to 300-Year Plan with GM Deal," Bloomberg LP, 2018, https://www.bloomberg.com/news/articles/2018-05-31/gm-driverless-car-deal-adds-to-softbank-chief-s-300-year-plan

[3] "The Yale Endowment 2017," 2017, https://static1.squarespace.com/static/55db7b87e4b0dca22fba2438/t/5a c5890e758d4611a98edd15/1522895146491/Yale_Endowment_17.pdf

[4] "A Solid Foundation for the Future," CalPERS, 2019, https://www.calpers.ca.gov/page/about/organization/facts-at-a-glance/solid-foundation-for-the-future

[5] Peters, James. "Public Employees' Retirement System Board of Administration Investment Committee Open Session," CalPERS, 2019, https://www.calpers.ca.gov/docs/board-agendas/201902/invest/transcript-ic_a.pdf

[6] "The Yale Endowment 2017," 2017, https://static1.squarespace.com/static/55db7b87e4b0dca22fba2438/t/5a c5890e758d4611a98edd15/1522895146491/Yale_Endowment_17.pdf

[7] Stafford, Erik. "Replicating Private Equity with Value Investing, Homemade Leverage, and Hold-to-Maturity Accounting," Harvard Business School, 2015, https://www.hbs.edu/faculty/Publication%20Files/ReplicatingPE_201512 _3859877f-bd53-4d3e-99aa-6daec2a3a2d3.pdf

[8] "Economic growth second-longest expansion on record," UNC Charlotte, 2019, https://inside.uncc.edu/news-features/2019-03-14/economic-growth-second-longest-expansion-record

[9] Carlson, Ben. "Be Wary of the Gap Between Stock and Bond Yields," Bloomberg Opinion, 2018, https://www.bloomberg.com/opinion/articles/2018-03-07/be-wary-of-the-gap-between-stock-and-bond-yields

[10] Buffett & Loomis. "Warren Buffett on The Stock Market," Fortune, 2001,
https://archive.fortune.com/magazines/fortune/fortune_archive/2001/12/10/314691/index.htm

[11] "Stock Market Capitalization to GDP for United States," FRED Economic Data, 2018,
https://fred.stlouisfed.org/series/DDDM01USA156NWDB

[12] "Online Data Robert Shiller," Yale, N.D.,
http://www.econ.yale.edu/~shiller/data.htm

[13] Makintosh, James. "Inverted Yield Curve Is Telling Investors What They Already Know," The Wall Street Journal, 2019,
https://www.wsj.com/articles/inverted-yield-curve-is-telling-investors-what-they-already-know-11553425200?mod=djemMoneyBeat_us&ns=prod/accounts-wsj

[14] IBM. "IBM To Acquire Red Hat, Completely Changing The Cloud Landscape And Becoming World's #1 Hybrid Cloud Provider," IBM Newsroom, 2018, https://newsroom.ibm.com/2018-10-28-IBM-To-Acquire-Red-Hat-Completely-Changing-The-Cloud-Landscape-And-Becoming-Worlds-1-Hybrid-Cloud-Provider

[15] Norris, Floyd. "Market Place; An Expert Shuns Risk Arbitrage" The New York Times, 1989,
https://www.nytimes.com/1989/03/28/business/market-place-an-expert-shuns-risk-arbitrage.html?mtrref=www.google.com&gwh=B71258B249C3D29F3980A93F9BBE4F6B&gwt=pay

[16] Stafford, Erik. "Replicating Private Equity with Value Investing, Homemade Leverage, and Hold-to-Maturity Accounting." Harvard Business School Working Paper, No. 16-081, January 2016.

[17] Franklin & Manjesh. "Blackstone buyout fund raises $22 billion, to set record: source," Journal Pioneer, 2019,
https://www.journalpioneer.com/business/business/blackstone-buyout-fund-raises-22-billion-to-set-record-source-297530/

[18] McCabe, Carrie. "Not Enough Private Equity to Go Around," Forbes, 2019, https://www.forbes.com/sites/carriemccabe/2019/03/28/not-enough-private-equity-to-go-around/#41ab515371ad

[19] Balchunas, Eric. "A Bear Market Would Be a Death Knell for Active Funds," Bloomberg Opinion, 2018,
https://www.bloomberg.com/opinion/articles/2018-05-03/a-bear-market-would-be-a-death-knell-for-active-funds

184

[20] Doskeland & Stromberg. "Evaluating Investments in Unlisted Equity for The Norwegian Government Pension Fund Global (Gpfg)." Stockholm School of Economics, 2018, https://www.regjeringen.no/contentassets/7fb88d969ba34ea6a0cd9225b28711a9/evaluating_doskelandstromberg_10012018.pdf

[21] Stafford, Erik. "Replicating Private Equity with Value Investing, Homemade Leverage, and Hold-to-Maturity Accounting," Harvard Business School, 2015, https://www.hbs.edu/faculty/Publication%20Files/ReplicatingPE_201512_3859877f-bd53-4d3e-99aa-6daec2a3a2d3.pdf

[22] Klymochko, Julian. "The Myth of Illiquidity Premium," Accelerate, 2019, https://accelerateshares.com/blog/the-myth-of-the-illiquidity-premium/

[23] Smith, Eric. "Equivalent of doping? Private equity takes juicing the numbers to the next level," Financial Times, 2019, https://www.ft.com/content/faa4406e-5f6c-11e9-b285-3acd5d43599e

[24] Gottfried, Miriam. "LBO Volume Surges as KKR, Others Put $1 Trillion Cash Pile to Work," The Wall Street Journal, 2018, https://www.wsj.com/articles/lbo-volume-surges-as-kkr-others-put-1-trillion-cash-pile-to-work-1528887600

[25] "The Yale Endowment," Yale University, 2018, https://static1.squarespace.com/static/55db7b87e4b0dca22fba2438/t/5c8b09008165f55d4bec1a36/1552615684090/2018+Yale+Endowment.pdf

[26] Thomas & Chuan-Yang. "The 52-Week High and Momentum Investing," The Journal of Finance, 2004, https://www.bauer.uh.edu/tgeorge/papers/gh4-paper.pdf

[27] Van Gelderen, Huij, & Kyosev. "Factor Investing from Concept to Implementation," SSRN, 2019, https://papers.ssrn.com/sol3/papers.cfm?abstract_id=3313364

[28] Ang, Andrew. "Factors making waves," BlackRock, 2018, https://www.blackrock.com/us/individual/investment-ideas/what-is-factor-investing/factor-commentary/andrews-angle/factor-growth

[29] Yardeni, Abbott, Quintana. "Stock Market Indicators: S&P 500 Buybacks & Dividends," Yardeni Research, 2019, https://www.yardeni.com/pub/buybackdiv.pdf

[30] "Morningstar® Document Research," Bp Prudhoe Bay Royalty Trust – Bpt, 2019,

http://app.quotemedia.com/data/downloadFiling?ref=12750962&type=PDF&symbol=BPT&companyName=BP+Prudhoe+Bay+Royalty+Trust&formType=10-K&formDescription=Annual+report+with+a+comprehensive+overview+of+the+company&dateFiled=2019-03-01

[31] Klymochko, Julian. "Whatever You Do, Don't Invest Based on Dividend Yield," Accelerate, 2019, https://accelerateshares.com/blog/whatever-you-do-dont-invest-based-on-dividend-yield/

[32] Klymochko, Julian. "Value Investing Is Dead! #FAKENEWS," Accelerate, 2019, https://accelerateshares.com/blog/value-investing-is-dead-fakenews/

[33] Imbert, Fred. "Berkshire shareholders go to Omaha to get as much Buffett and Munger as they can," CNBC, 2018, https://www.cnbc.com/2018/05/05/shareholders-try-to-get-as-much-buffett-and-munger-as-they-can.html

[34] "Bret "Hit Man" Hart: The Best There Is, the Best There Was, the Best There Ever Will Be," Wikipedia, 2019, https://en.wikipedia.org/wiki/Bret_%22Hit_Man%22_Hart:_The_Best_There_Is,_the_Best_There_Was,_the_Best_There_Ever_Will_Be

[35] "Birkshire Hathaway Inc. 2017 Annual Report," 2017, http://www.berkshirehathaway.com/2017ar/2017ar.pdf

[36] Zweig, Jason. "When Charlie Munger Calls, Listen and Learn," The Wall Street Journal, 2019, https://www.wsj.com/articles/when-charlie-munger-calls-listen-and-learn-11548421209

About the Author

Julian is the CEO and Chief Investment Officer of Accelerate Financial Technologies Inc. Prior to founding Accelerate in February 2018, Julian was the Chief Investment Officer of Ross Smith Asset Management where he managed award-winning alternative investment strategies for nearly a decade. He founded and managed a top performing Canadian alternative fund in 2017. Julian also managed a 6-time award winning market neutral hedge fund and founded an award-winning event-driven arbitrage fund. Prior to Ross Smith Asset Management, he was an Analyst at BMO Capital Markets. He attended the University of Manitoba where he graduated with a Bachelor of Science (Engineering) and a Bachelor of Commerce (Finance). Julian is a Chartered Financial Analyst (CFA) charterholder.

Julian is the host of the Absolute Return Podcast. He has appeared on Bloomberg, BNN, and other global and national media.

Made in the USA
Middletown, DE
26 December 2019